"Where are the Spurgeons of this generation?" So R. Albert Mohler concludes his call for expositional preaching in today's pulpits. Thank God that the man occupying the position of the president of The Southern Baptist Theological Seminary would write such a book as this! Deeply theological, concerned and confident, this is a clearly written book with an important message on THE crucial topic for churches and preachers today.

—MARK DEVER, senior pastor, Capitol Hill Baptist Church, Washington, DC and founder of 9Marks

This book shows a side of Dr. Mohler that many don't see. In addition to his roles as a seminary president, discerning observer of culture, and evangelical spokesman, Dr. Mohler excels as a preacher, passionate about God's Word and confident in its power to save. *He Is Not Silent: Preaching in a Postmodern World* instructs us in, and urges upon us, a view of preaching that is theologically profound, culturally aware, pastorally sensitive, and spiritually edifying. Evangelical pastors desperately need the clear, confident, and urgent plea that issues from these pages.

—C. J. MAHANEY
president, Sovereign Grace Ministries

I preach because nothing else can satisfy the urgency and passion that God has ignited in my heart for His truth and His people. The same should be true for you. If you can go sell cars or shuffle stocks instead of being a pastor and preacher of God's Word, then go do that. For the rest of us, I'm grateful for my friend and mentor, Al Mohler, who dares us to think beyond seminary syllabi and safe homiletics. Careful—this book can change your ministry.

—JAMES MACDONALD, senior pastor, Harvest Bible Chapel
Bible Teacher, Walk in the Word

Albert Mohler is one of North America's most trenchant, incisive analysts of Christianity and culture. In this passionate book, he makes a persuasive case for the kind of preaching that our culture needs: the faithful exposition of Holy Scripture, in which the triune God speaks His own life-giving gospel for the salvation of sinners and the sanctification of his people.

—PHILIP GRAHAM RYKEN
senior minister, Tenth Presbyterian Church
Bible Teacher, Every Last Word

As President of The Southern Baptist Theological Seminary, Dr. Al Mohler trains thousands of pastors and ministers to proclaim the Word of God with integrity and clarity. The book you hold is the result of a lifetime of challenging and developing effective biblical preachers. I predict it will become a classic for the preparation and delivery of sermons that exalt Christ and strengthen God's church for generations to come.

—DR. JACK GRAHAM
pastor, Prestonwood Baptist Church, Plano, Texas

"According to the Bible, exposition is preaching. And preaching is exposition." Dr. Al Mohler's statement pretty well sums up this powerful volume on the theology of preaching. I wish every young man called to preach could be given a copy of this excellent volume on the necessity of expository preaching. It can transform any pastor's preaching ministry. Wouldn't hurt preachers of any age to read this one!

—JERRY VINES, pastor emeritus, First Baptist Church,
Jacksonville, FL and president of Jerry Vines Ministries, Inc.

"Mohler at his best. Chapter 7 alone is worth the price of the book!"
—Alistair Begg
senior minister, Parkside Church, Cleveland, OH

HE IS NOT SILENT

PREACHING IN A
POSTMODERN WORLD

R. ALBERT MOHLER JR.

MOODY PUBLISHERS
CHICAGO

All Scripture quotations, unless otherwise indicated, are taken from *The Holy Bible,
English Standard Version*. Copyright © 2000, 2001 by Crossway Bibles, a division of
Good News Publishers. Used by permission. All rights reserved.

Scripture quotations marked NASB are taken from the *New American Standard Bible*®,
Copyright © 1960, 1962, 1963, 1968, 1971, 1972, 1973, 1975, 1977, 1995 by The
Lockman Foundation. Used by permission. (www.Lockman.org)

Scripture quotations marked NIV are taken from the *Holy Bible, New International Version*®. NIV®. Copyright © 1973, 1978, 1984 by International Bible Society. Used by
permission of Zondervan. All rights reserved.

Published in association with the literary agency of Wolgemuth & Associates, Inc.

Editor: Jim Vincent
Interior Design: Ragont Design
Cover Design: Brand Navigation

Library of Congress Cataloging-in-Publication Data

Mohler, R. Albert, 1959-
    He is not silent : preaching in a postmodern world / R. Albert Mohler.
        p. cm.
    Includes bibliographical references.
    ISBN 978-0-8024-5489-8
    1. Preaching. 2. Bible—Homiletical use. 3. Postmodernism—Religious
aspects—Christianity. I. Title.

BV4211.3.M64 2008
251—dc22

                                                                      2008020862

We hope you enjoy this book from Moody Publishers. Our goal is to provide high-qual-
ity, thought-provoking books and products that connect truth to your real needs and
challenges. For more information on other books and products written and produced
from a biblical perspective, go to www.moodypublishers.com or write to:

Moody Publishers
820 N. LaSalle Boulevard
Chicago, IL 60610

1 3 5 7 9 10 8 6 4 2

Printed in the United States of America

To the pastors of my boyhood

T. Rupert Coleman
Southside Baptist Church
Lakeland, Florida

Robert L. Smith
First Baptist Church
Pompano Beach, Florida

To our pastor

Kevin Ezell
Highview Baptist Church
Louisville, Kentucky

And to all the faithful Servants of the Word
who are preaching the Word,
in season and out of season,
known and unknown to the world,
known to the faithful and to God.

CONTENTS

ACKNOWLEDGMENTS

This book has emerged out of an intense concern for the state of preaching in the church, and it has taken shape in the course of much thinking, reflecting, teaching, and preaching. Throughout that entire process, the work has been strengthened and enriched through countless conversations and through engagement with others who share this concern as well as a sense of the glory of preaching as the first mark of the authentic church.

I am especially endebted to Dr. John MacArthur, Dr. Mark Dever, Dr. Ligon Duncan, Dr. John Piper, Dr. Hershael York, Dr. Danny Akin, Dr. Russell Moore, C. J. Mahaney, Dr. James Merritt, Dr. Robert Vogel, John Stott, the late Dr. James Montgomery Boice, and other preachers who stayed up late into the night talking about expository preaching.

This project would never have taken its present shape without the service of Greg Gilbert in my office, who has directed his fine editorial eye to this manuscript, and has devoted himself to it because of his own passion for biblical preaching. My sadness in his leaving to assume new responsibilities elsewhere is surpassed only by my pride in the fact that he is going to be a pastor—the highest of callings. He will preach faithfully and he will preach well.

A team of others at Southern Seminary, most notably Jason Allen, Russell Moore, Doug Walker, and Dan Dumas, make my attention to projects like this possible. I also want to thank the great team at Moody Publishers and my representative, Robert Wolgemuth, who has believed in this project from the start.

Finally, I write this with the full knowledge that nothing I can ever accomplish in this life is without the grand contribution of my wife, Mary, whose devoted love to me makes all that I do richer, better, and more faithful. As always, our children, Katie and Christopher, helped make life more joyous, more urgent, more lively, and more humorous. Who can put a price on that?

FOREWORD

One of the clearest lessons we learn from church history is that strong biblical preaching is absolutely vital to the health and vitality of the church. From the birth of the New Testament church until today, every significant phase of authentic revival, reformation, missionary expansion, or robust church growth has also been an era of *biblical preaching*.

The preaching of God's Word was of course one of the hallmarks of the apostolic age. The most influential post-apostolic church fathers, including all the early apologists, were also bold and powerful preachers of Scripture. Early theologians such as Tertullian, Jerome, and Augustine were likewise skilled preachers as well as brilliant biblical scholars. The leading men among the Lollards, the magisterial reformers, and the Puritans were some of the finest, most courageous expository preachers the world has ever known. The Great Awakenings, the Welsh Revivals, and the early student missionary movements were all ignited by the powerful preaching of biblical doctrine.

No wonder. Scripture says preaching is the primary means God chose to save those who believe (1 Corinthians 1:21). Preaching is also the main vehicle the Holy Spirit has chosen through which to feed and instruct the church corporately (1 Corinthians 2:1–16). And the Word of God itself furnishes the only valid substance of any preacher's message (2 Timothy 4:2–4).

It is no accident that the church was originally born and unleashed into the first-century world chiefly through preaching. In fact, almost every time Luke made note of growth patterns in the early church, he expressed it in terms like this: "*The word of God* kept on spreading" (Acts 6:7; cf. 12:4 and 19:20). Clearly, preaching—specifically *biblical* preaching—is the main strategy God Himself ordained for church growth and for leading and feeding His flock. Naturally, it is the one strategy He has always truly blessed.

It is remarkable, then, that over the past half century (or longer) evangelicals have devoted vast quantities of energy and resources to the invention of novel church-growth strategies that tend to discount biblical preaching. Such schemes sometimes even deliberately avoid any reference to the Bible altogether—especially when unbelievers are present. They aim instead at attracting people through marketing campaigns, entertainments, social activities, and other similar techniques. Many of today's evangelical church leaders have borrowed their management philosophies from the corporate world; they have taken their fashion cues from the entertainment industry; they have imitated the communications styles of secular mass media (favoring sound-bites over substance); and they have employed various bells and whistles from modern technology designed mainly to amaze and impress rather than to teach and edify. The visible church now mirrors the world to a disturbing degree. A major portion of Christendom is spiritually starved—and sound, biblical preaching has become an extremely rare commodity.

There are several encouraging signs that the tide may be turning. Christians hungry for the Word of God are pleading for their churches to recover the priority of faithful, in-depth, biblical preaching and teaching. (I hear from people all over the country every week asking for recommendations of churches where the Bible is seriously preached.) Many young men now entering ministry have a fresh commitment to preaching the Word of God, and they are being trained and equipped to become true expositors rather than showmen and motivational speakers.

Al Mohler stands at the head of a handful of men in his generation who are helping renew, stimulate, and feed the church's appetite for expository preaching. As a seminary president, his driving passion is to equip young men and send them out to preach the Word of God. His courageous leadership is a model to his students, and his accomplishments already have been legendary. But I'm confident his long-term legacy will be even more profound and far-reaching—mainly because of what he has done and is doing to restore biblical preaching to its rightful place in Baptist churches.

Dr. Mohler is a careful student of preaching—and a fine preacher in his own right. He is supremely gifted with an extraordinary ability to blend meticulous scholarship with deep spiritual passion. He has been a mainstay for many years in our annual Shepherds' Conferences, with a solid and well-deserved reputation for sound doctrine, bold clarity, and (above all) a fervent commitment to biblical exposition. A few years ago, when the elders of Grace Community Church were planning a celebration for my thirty-fifth anniversary as their senior pastor, they decided it should be a day of preaching. They wanted to focus on the biblical mandate for church leaders to preach the Word, and they wanted a great preacher to lead the event. Dr. Mohler was their first choice, and he was absolutely the *right* choice. His message that day stirred our hearts and gave us a fresh commitment to remain at the task God has called us to do.

That's why I am so glad to see this book. Dr. Mohler's passion for preaching is infectious. His diagnosis of what ails contemporary preaching is spot-on, and his suggestions for what to do about it are full of insight and challenge. My prayer is that this volume will be widely read by preachers and lay people alike, and that it will be used by the Lord to help turn a generation of faithful believers (and countless churches as well) away from all that is trivial and worldly—and back to what really matters.

—John MacArthur

PREFACE
The State of Preaching Today

It was the best of times, it was the worst of times, it was the age of wisdom, it was the age of foolishness, it was the epoch of belief, it was the epoch of incredulity . . ." With those famous words, Charles Dickens introduced his great novel *A Tale of Two Cities.* Of course, Dickens had the two cities of London and Paris in mind, and much of his story revealed that the tenor of the times depended upon where one lived.

To a large degree, that remains true as we consider the state of preaching today. Whether it is the best of times or the worst of times depends largely upon where one chooses to look.

On the one hand, there are signs of great promise and encouragement. For example, a large number of younger evangelical pastors today are unabashedly committed to biblical exposition. They represent a resurgence of genuine biblical exposition from the pulpits of churches situated in every part of the country, from the inner city to the suburbs and beyond. This new generation is proving once again that the effective and faithful exposition of the Word of God draws persons to Christ and leads to spiritual growth and to the health of the church. Indeed this generation of young ministers, along with others making their way through college and seminary education, may point toward a renaissance of biblical preaching in coming years.

On the other hand, the last few decades have been a period of wanton experimentation in many pulpits. One of the most troubling developments is the decline and eclipse of expository preaching. Numerous influential voices within evangelicalism are suggesting that the age of the expository sermon is now past. In its place, some contemporary preachers now substitute messages intentionally designed to reach secular or superficial congregations—messages that avoid preaching a biblical text and thus avoid a potentially embarrassing confrontation with biblical truth.

How did this happen? Given the central place of preaching in the New Testament church, it would seem that the priority of biblical preaching should be uncontested. After all, as John A. Broadus, one of the Southern Baptist Theological Seminary's founding faculty, famously remarked, "Preaching is characteristic of Christianity. No other religion has made the regular and frequent assembling of groups of people, to hear religious instruction and exhortation, an integral part of divine worship."[1]

I believe the weakening of preaching at the beginning of the twenty-first century is the result of several factors, all of which are matters of genuine concern, and all of which have worked together to undermine the role of preaching in the church and to redefine it as something other than the exposition and application of the biblical text.

First, contemporary preaching suffers from a loss of confidence in the power of the word.

Contemporary Americans are surrounded by more words than any previous generation in human history. We are bombarded with words delivered to us in every conceivable form—sung, broadcast, electrified, printed, and spoken. Words have been digitalized, commercialized, and subjected to postmodern linguistic theories.

Taken together, all this amounts to a significant loss of confidence in the word as written and spoken. Several years ago, the photographer Richard Avedon declared that "images are fast replacing words as our primary language." Similarly, in *The Rise of the Image, the Fall of the Word*, author Mitchell Stephens of New York University argues that "the image is replacing the word as the predominant means of mental transport."

Since preaching is itself a form of "mental transport," any loss of confidence in the word leads to a loss of confidence in preaching. Ultimately, preaching will cease to be *Christian* preaching if the preacher loses confidence in the authority of the Bible as the Word of God and in the power of the spoken word to communicate the saving and transforming message of the Bible. The preacher must stand up and speak with confidence, declaring the Word of God to a congregation that is bombarded with hundreds of thousands of words each week, many of them delivered with a sound track or moving images. The audacious claim of Christian preaching is that the faithful declaration of the Word of God, spoken through the preacher's voice, is even more powerful than anything music or image can deliver.

Second, contemporary preaching suffers from an infatuation with technology.

The French philosopher Jacques Ellul was truly prophetic when he pointed to the rise of technology and technique as one of the greatest challenges to Christian faithfulness in our times. We live in a day of technological hubris and the ubiquity of technological assistance. We are engaged in few tasks, physical or mental, that are now unassisted by some form of technology. For most of us, the use of these technologies comes with little attentiveness to how the technology reshapes the task and the experience. The same is true for preachers who have rushed to incorporate visual technology and media in the preaching event.

The effort is no doubt well intended, driven by a missiological concern to reach persons whose primary form of "mental transport" has become visual. Thus, preachers use clips from films, dynamic graphics, and other eye-catching technologies to gain and hold the congregation's attention. But the danger of this approach is seen in the fact that the visual quickly overcomes the verbal. Beyond this, the visual is often directed toward a very narrow slice of human experience, particularly focused on the affective and emotional aspects of our perception. Movies *move* us by the skillful manipulation of emotion, driven by sound track and manipulated by skillful directing techniques.

This is exactly where the preacher must not go. The power of the Word of God, spoken through the human voice, is seen in the Bible's unique power to penetrate all dimensions of the human personality. As God made clear, even in the Ten Commandments, He has chosen to be *heard* and not *seen*. The use of visual technologies threatens to confuse this basic fact of biblical faith.

Third, contemporary preaching suffers from embarrassment before the biblical text.

Over the years, I have heard innumerable sermons from evangelical preachers, and I cannot help but notice that some have a tendency to appear rather embarrassed before the biblical text. The persistent attacks upon biblical authority and the sensitivities of our times have taken a toll on the preacher's confidence in the actual text of the Bible.

On the theological left, the answer is quite simple—just discard the text and write it off as patriarchal, oppressive, and completely unacceptable in light of an updated concept of God. Among evangelicals, we can be thankful that fewer preachers are willing to dismiss or discard the text as sub-biblical or warped by ancient prejudices. But even so, many of these preachers simply disregard and ignore vast sections of Scripture, focusing instead on texts that are more comfortable, palatable, and nonconfrontational to the modern mind. This is a form of pastoral neglect and malpractice, corrected only by a comprehensive embrace of the Bible—all of it—as the inspired, inerrant, and authoritative Word of God. *All* of it is for our good. As Paul said to Timothy, "*All* Scripture is breathed out by God and profitable" for us (2 Timothy 3:16, italics added).

Fourth, contemporary preaching suffers from an emptying of biblical content.

The last point was concerned with passages of Scripture that are never preached, but what about the texts that are preached? Are today's preachers actually studying for the content of the passage? In far too many cases, it seems that the text becomes a point of departure for some message—again, no doubt well intended—which the pastor wishes to share with the congregation. Beyond this, the text of Scripture is often emptied—evacuated—of biblical content when, regardless of a passage's textual form or context, the content is uniformly presented as a set of pithy "points" that come together in a staple outline form.

Every text does have a point, of course, and the preacher's main concern should be to communicate that central truth. In fact, he should design the sermon to serve that overarching purpose. Furthermore, the content of the passage is to be applied to life—but application must be determined by exposition, not vice versa.

Another problem that leads to an evacuation of biblical content is a loss of the "big picture" of Scripture. Far too many preachers give inadequate attention to the canonical context of the passage to be preached and of its place in the overarching story of God's purpose to glorify Himself through the redemption of sinners. Taken out of context, and without clear attention to biblical theology, preaching becomes a series of disconnected talks on disconnected texts. This falls far short of the glory of true biblical preaching.

Fifth, contemporary preaching suffers from a focus on felt needs.

The current debate over preaching is most commonly explained as an argument about the focus and shape of the sermon. Should the preacher seek to preach a biblical text through an expository sermon? Or should the preacher direct the sermon to the "felt needs" and perceived concerns of the hearers?

Harry Emerson Fosdick, pastor of the Riverside Church in New York City and perhaps the most famous (or infamous) preacher of the twentieth century's early decades, once defined the task of preaching like this: "Preaching is personal counseling on a group basis." Earlier evangelicals recognized Fosdick's approach as a rejection of biblical preaching. An unabashed theological liberal, Fosdick paraded his rejection of biblical inspiration, inerrancy, and infallibility—and rejected other doctrines central to the Christian faith. Enamored with trends in psychological theory, Fosdick became liberal Protestantism's happy pulpit therapist. The goal of his preaching was well captured by the title of one of his many books, *On Being a Real Person.*

Shockingly, this approach is now evident in many evangelical pulpits. Urged on by devotees of "needs-based preaching," many evangelicals have abandoned the text without recognizing that they have done so. These preachers may eventually get to the text in the course of the sermon, but the text does not set the agenda or establish the shape of the message. The sacred desk has become an advice center, and the pew has become the therapist's couch. Psychological and practical concerns have displaced theological exegesis, and the preacher directs his sermon to the congregation's perceived needs rather than to their need for a Savior.

The problem, of course, is that the sinner does not know what his most urgent need is. He is blind to his need for redemption and reconciliation with God, and focuses on potentially real but temporal needs such as personal fulfillment, financial security, family peace, and career advancement. Too many sermons settle for answering these expressed needs and concerns and fail to proclaim the Word of Truth.

Sixth, contemporary preaching suffers from an absence of gospel.

The preaching of the apostles *always* presented the *kerygma*—the heart of the gospel. The clear presentation of the gospel must be a part of the sermon, no matter the text. As Charles Spurgeon expressed this so eloquently, preach the Word, place it in its canonical context, and "make a bee-line to the cross."

The approach of many preachers is to present helpful and practical messages, often with generalized Christian content but without any clear presentation of the gospel or call to decision and accountability to the text or to the claims of Christ. The apostles should be our model here, consistently preaching the death, burial, and resurrection of Jesus Christ. Of course, in order for the gospel to make sense, authentic preaching must also deal honestly with the reality of human sin and must do so with a candor equal to that of the biblical text. All this presents the preacher with some significant challenges in our age of "sensitivities." But in the end, preaching devoid of this content—preaching that evades the biblical text and biblical truth—falls short of anything we can rightly call *Christian* preaching.

These are indeed the best of times and the worst of times. I am thankful for a renaissance of expository preaching, especially among many young preachers. I am thankful for stalwart pulpit examples who now serve as mentors to a generation hungry to see how biblical exposition constitutes the very center of effective and powerful ministry, and for a number of outstanding programs in seminaries directed toward encouraging and equipping this generation for that task.

At the same time, I am also concerned that dangerous trends and many popular examples threaten to undermine the centrality of biblical exposition in evangelical pulpits. In the end, the Christian preacher simply must confront the congregation with the Word of God. That confrontation will be at times awkward, challenging, and difficult. After all, this is the Word that pierces us like a sword. The evangelical preacher must set his aim at letting the sword loose, neither hiding it nor dulling its edge.

CHAPTER 1

PREACHING AS WORSHIP

The Heart of Christian Worship

The subject of worship is now one of the most controversial issues in the local congregation, if a survey of the literature on worship, and the conversations currently taking place among the churches are true indicators. In fact, many current book titles in evangelical publishing suggest that what the church faces today is "worship warfare." That very phrase—the combination of the words *worship* and *war*—should lead us to very sincere and sober reflection.

It is true that worship has led to some warfare. In local congregations we see not only confusion but also fighting, controversy, and splitting. And what is the meaning of all this? My concern is that the issue of worship will define not only our church services but also our theology and our beliefs about God. There is no more important issue for the church of the Lord Jesus Christ than that we worship God as He Himself would have us to worship.

And just how do we do that? Most evangelicals would quickly

agree that worship is central to the life of the church, but beyond that, there would be no consensus to several unavoidable questions: What is worship? And what does God desire that we should do in worship? Though most evangelicals mention the preaching of the Word as a necessary or customary part of worship, the prevailing model of worship in evangelical churches is increasingly defined by music, along with innovations such as drama and video presentations. Preaching has in large part retreated, and a host of entertaining innovations have taken its place.

Any consideration of Christian preaching must begin with the realization that *preaching is essentially an act of worship*. Therefore, to understand what is required of us as preachers, we must first understand what it means to worship. The Lord Himself reminded us that God seeks those worshipers who will worship Him in spirit and truth (John 4:23). But what does it mean to worship God in spirit? What does it mean to worship Him in truth? And how does preaching fit into all that?

LINKING WORSHIP WITH THEOLOGY

Worshiping God in truth is fundamentally a matter of theology. Yet theology is by definition not an ivory-tower discipline. It is not merely a form of academic discourse. When rightly conducted, theology is the conversation of the people of God seeking to understand the Lord whom we worship and to know how He wills to be worshiped. Geoffrey Wainwright of Duke University made this point poignantly when he entitled his systematic theology book *Doxology*. Theology and worship are inextricably linked.

Thus we should be reminded that the purpose of the theologian— and the preacher—is to serve the church so that the people of God worship Him more faithfully. By understanding God's revelation in His Word, we know how He would wish to be worshiped. So we might ask in that light, what are the proper conditions of evangelical worship? Those persons who claim to be established in the gospel and submitted to the Word of God, how should they worship?

We know the history of worship through the ages. We know what took place in the Reformation and what transpired in the English reforms. We know what took place as features were stripped away that were considered to be unbiblical, and yet now in so many ways we see those same things returning. What is the condition of evangelical worship today? In answer to that question, it is not an exaggeration to suggest words such as *pandemonium, confusion*, and *consternation*.

In the midst of the upheaval, there is a great deal of perspective to be found from reading the late A. W. Tozer. This is what he said some decades ago:

> We have the breezy, self-confident Christians with little affinity for Christ and His cross. We have the joy-bell boys that can bounce out there and look as much like a game show host as possible. Yet, they are doing it for Jesus' sake?! The hypocrites! They're not doing it for Jesus' sake at all; they are doing it in their own carnal flesh and are using the church as a theater because they haven't yet reached the place where the legitimate theater would take them.[1]

Tozer takes his argument further:

> It is now common practice in most evangelical churches to offer the people, especially the young people, a maximum of entertainment and a minimum of serious instruction. It is scarcely possible in most places to get anyone to attend meeting where the only attraction is God. One can only conclude that God's professed children are bored with Him, for they must be wooed to meeting with a stick of striped candy in the form of religious movies, games and refreshments.
>
> This has influenced the whole pattern of church life, and even brought into being a new type of church architecture designed to house the golden calf.
>
> So we have the strange anomaly of orthodoxy in creed and

heterodoxy in practice. The striped-candy technique has been so fully integrated into our present religious thinking that it is simply taken for granted. Its victims never dream that it is not a part of the teachings of Christ and His apostles.

Any objection to the carryings-on of our present golden calf Christianity is met with the triumphant reply, "But we are winning them!" And winning them to what? To true discipleship? To cross-carrying? To self-denial? To separation from the world? To crucifixion of the flesh? To holy living? To nobility of character? To a despising of the world's treasures? To hard self-discipline? To love for God? To total commital to Christ? Of course, the answer to all these questions is "no."[2]

These words were written several decades ago, but Tozer certainly saw the future.

BEING CAREFUL NOT TO CORRUPT OUR WORSHIP

Kent Hughes, senior pastor emeritus of College Church in Wheaton, Illinois, has also written perceptively on this issue. Hughes put it this way:

The unspoken but increasingly common assumption of today's Christendom is that worship is primarily for us—to meet our needs. Such worship services are entertainment focused, and the worshipers are uncommitted spectators who are silently grading the performance. From this perspective preaching becomes a homiletics of consensus—preaching to felt needs—man's conscious agenda instead of God's. Such preaching is always topical and never textual. Biblical information is minimized, and the sermons are short and full of stories. Anything and everything that is suspected of making the marginal attender uncomfortable is removed from the service. . . . Taken to the nth degree, this philosophy instills a tragic self-centeredness. That is, everything is judged by how it affects man. This terribly corrupts one's theology.[3]

Hughes is right. Our confused worship corrupts our theology, and our weak theology corrupts our worship. Are these voices alarmist? They do mean to sound an alarm. But there are many others who are saying, "Don't worry. Be happy. Go worship." One recent church growth author has written:

> Does God care how He is worshiped?

> Worship is like a car to get us from where we are to where God wants us to be. Transportation and communication are imperative; the mode or vehicle is not imperative. Some worship God in cathedrals with the rich traditional organ tones of Bach and Feuer from the classics of Europe. They travel in a Mercedes Benz. Some worship God in simple wooden churches with a steeple pointing heavenward. They sing the gospel songs of Charles Wesley or Fanny Cosby. They travel in a Ford or Chevy. Some worship God with the contemporary sounds of praise music with a gentle beat. They travel in a convertible sports coupe. Some worship God to the whine of a guitar and the amplifiers to the max. They travel on a motorcycle, without a muffler.[4]

But surely there is more to worship than the spectrum of taste from a Mercedes Benz to a motorcycle. There must be something weightier here. "Worship is like a car to get us from where we are to where God wants us to be." Can that be said with a straight face as we listen to the Scripture speak of worship?

We know from the onset that there are many different Christian opinions concerning worship. This does not come to us as news. But the real issue is whether God Himself has an opinion on this issue. Does God care how He is worshiped? Or is He some kind of *laissez-faire* deity who cares not how His people worship Him but instead is happy with the hope that some people somewhere will worship Him in some way?

Scripture reveals that God in fact does care how His people worship Him. Leviticus 10:1–3 (NASB) serves as a witness to this point.

> Now Nadab and Abihu, the sons of Aaron, took their respective firepans, and after putting fire in them, placed incense on it and offered strange fire before the Lord, which He had not commanded them. And fire came out from the presence of the Lord and consumed them, and they died before the Lord. Then Moses said to Aaron, "It is what the Lord spoke, saying, 'By those who come near Me I will be treated as holy, and before all the people I will be honored.'"

Nadab and Abihu were Aaron's sons. They were priests and so had every right to offer sacrifices to God in worship. But they did what God had not commanded them to do. They brought strange fire to the altar, and because of that they were consumed. Clearly then, God does have an opinion about worship. He is a jealous God—a God who loves us, but a God who also instructs and commands His people to worship Him rightly.

Scripture makes clear that worship is something we do, not just something we *attend*. It is not merely an issue for the pastor and other ministers, nor for the musicians and those who plan the service. Worship is an issue for the entire congregation, for worship is something we do together. It is our corporate and common responsibility to worship God as He desires.

A PATTERN FOR WORSHIP FROM GOD'S WORD

Where then shall we turn for instruction on how we ought to worship? There is only one place we can turn, and that is to the Word of God. The norm of our worship must be the Word of God, the Word that He Himself has spoken. As we turn to this Word, we see a pattern of acceptable worship, a pattern that is repeated throughout the fabric of Scripture from beginning to end. Scripture is, as the Reformers confessed, *norma ormans non normata*, "the norm of norms which cannot be normed." That is what we mean when we say *"sola scriptura"* —that Scripture is the norm of our worship. There is nothing external to Scripture that can "norm" or correct it.

Scripture itself sets the terms, and so we turn to the Bible to learn how God would have us worship.

HOW AUTHENTIC WORSHIP BEGINS: A TRUE VISION OF THE LIVING GOD

In Isaiah 6:1–8, we are given a picture of authentic worship, one that teaches us what God expects of His people when they worship Him. First of all, the prophet Isaiah experienced a theophany, a vision of the true and living God. And if we are to worship God as He would have us to worship, we also must see God as He is. Right worship begins with a vision of the one true and living God.

Isaiah recounts that it was in the year of King Uzziah's death that he saw the Lord sitting on a throne, lofty and exalted, with the train of His robe filling the temple. The throne is a symbol of kingship and sovereignty, indicating that the one who sits upon it is both king and judge. It represents both power and righteousness. But there is even more, for the One whose train filled the temple is not alone. Verse 2 tells us that "above him stood the seraphim. Each had six wings: with two he covered his face, and with two he covered his feet, and with two he flew." The six wings of these seraphim—which literally means "burning ones" —convey a great deal of symbolism.

> He is what we are not. We are finite; He is infinite.

The wings with which they covered their faces must certainly indicate humility, while the covering of the feet represents purity. The seraphim knew in whose presence they were, and they dared not look into His face.

These winged creatures are not merely flying, hovering there in silence. They call out to one another, saying, "Holy, Holy, Holy, is the Lord of hosts. The whole earth is full of His glory!" Those words— "Holy, Holy, Holy"—are known as the "trisagion." In the Hebrew language there is no adequate comparative or superlative form, so repetition is used in this way in order to make a point. This thrice-repeated pattern occurs again in Revelation 4:8–11: "And the four living creatures, each one of them having six wings, are full of eyes around and within; and day and night they do not cease to say, Holy, Holy, Holy is the Lord God, the Almighty, who was and who is and who is to come" (NASB). The early church saw in this pattern a reference to the Trinity, and looking back with New Testament eyes, we can certainly understand that affirmation. But the central point of this construction seems to be one of emphasis.

Take Genesis 14:10, for example, where the original Hebrew speaks of someone falling into a "pit-pit." That construction may be translated as a "deep and great pit." It is one thing to fall into a pit, but it is quite another to fall into a "pit-pit"! The point is that when the seraphim call out, "Holy, Holy, Holy," they are declaring God's essence, identity, and being in terms of an all-surpassing holiness.

The holiness of God refers to His separateness from His creation. He is what we are not. We are finite; He is infinite. In other words, God is transcendent, and His holiness reveals the difference and the infinite contrast between His nature and ours. J. Alec Motyer defines holiness as "God's total and unique moral majesty." What a wonderful expression! God's moral majesty is complete and without rival. E. J. Young similarly suggests that holiness is the entirety of the divine perfection that separates God from His creation. That which is almost beyond our definition is what makes God, God. Holiness includes all God's attributes. His holiness is what defines Him.

I wonder if the vision of God held by so many who come to worship is anything like what the seraphim are telling us here. Do we worship with the understanding that God is holy and that "the whole earth is full of His glory"? I fear not. I wonder if in our worship we encounter anything like this vision of God. Do those who come to our services of worship come face-to-face with the reality of God? Or do they go away with a vision of some lesser God, some dehydrated deity? Worship is the people of God gathering together to confess His worthiness, His "worth-ship." How can we do that if we do not make clear who God is? Our very pattern of worship must testify to the character of God.

> Would an observer have any idea of the God of the Bible from our worship?

Worship has both objective and subjective components. Certainly worship is subjective. There is a personal, individual experience to be had in worship. But Scripture also makes clear that the subjective experience of worship must be predicated on the objective truth of the true and living God, the God who has revealed Himself in Scripture.

Roger Scruton, a well-known British philosopher, has suggested that worship is the most important indicator of what a person or group of people really believes about God. He writes: "God is defined in the act of worship far more precisely than he is defined by any theology."[5] In other words, if you want to know what a people really believe about God, don't spend time reading their theologians. Watch them worship. Listen to what they sing and to how they pray. Then you will know what they believe about this God whom they worship.

I am haunted by the thought that in the average evangelical church, the God of the Bible would never be known by watching us worship. Instead, what we have in so many churches is "McWorship" of a "McDeity." But what kind of God is that superficial, that weightless, and that insignificant? Would an observer have any idea of the God of the Bible from our worship? I wonder at times if this is an accidental development, or if it is an intentional evasion.

George Hunter III suggests that a thriving church must practice "celebrative worship." He offers two reasons: "1) To provide a celebration to which pre-Christians can relate and find meaning. 2) To remove the cringe factor by providing a service our people would love to invite their friends to, rather than a service they would dread inviting their friends to."[6] Here is a fascinating reversal. The purpose of celebrative worship, first, is to provide "a celebration to which pre-Christians can relate." But, second, he suggests removing anything he identifies as "the cringe factor" by providing a service to which our people would love to invite their friends, not one where the thought of inviting their friends would lead to a feeling of dread.

But isn't there a great deal of the *cringe factor* in Scripture? If you are going to remove the cringe factor from Scripture, then you are going to end up with a very thin book. Hebrews 10:31 reveals that "it is a terrifying thing to fall into the hands of the living God" (NASB). I wonder if there is anything that could even be remotely described as "terrifying" about the God we present in our "cringeless" worship. Just look at the decline of majesty and awe in evangelical hymnody. There we see a surrender of conviction and accommodation to the culture, which is really nothing less than a "dumbing down" of the contents of our songs. We have gone from "Holy, Holy, Holy" to "God the Swell Fellow."

And what is the result of this kind of accommodated Christianity? I quote Tozer again:

We have simplified until Christianity amounts to this: God is love; Jesus died for you; believe, accept, be jolly, have fun and tell others. And away we go—that is the Christianity of our day. I would not give a plug nickel for the whole business of it. Once in a while God has a poor bleeding sheep that manages to live on that kind of thing and we wonder how.[7]

True worship begins with a vision of the God of the Bible—a vision of the one true and living God.

WHERE AUTHENTIC WORSHIP LEADS:
CONFESSION OF SIN

Not only does authentic worship begin with a true vision of the living God, but second, authentic worship leads to a confession of sin, both individual and corporate. This is also clear in Isaiah 6:5 (NASB). Seeing God on His throne, Isaiah said, "Woe is me, for I am ruined! For I am a man of unclean lips, and I live among a people of unclean lips. Because my eyes have seen the King, the Lord of hosts." Isaiah was "undone" when he saw the true and living God in His holiness. He came to know the majestic, moral nature of this God, and he came to see God's righteousness and holiness. In dong so, Isaiah automatically saw his own utter sinfulness. He could not understand himself as anything but a sinner who was undone, dissolved, silenced. He saw himself doomed to die.

I want to suggest that this must happen in our worship as well. If we do not come face-to-face with our sin as individuals and as a congregation, we have not seen God, and we have not worshiped Him. For when we meet God in worship, we see ourselves as God sees us. We see ourselves as sinners. Psalm 51:1–4 models this kind of confession:

> Be gracious to me, O God, according to Your lovingkindness; according to the greatness of Your compassion blot out my transgressions. Wash me thoroughly from my iniquity and cleanse me from my sin. For I know my transgressions, and my sin is ever before me. Against You, You only, I have sinned and done what is evil in Your sight, so that You are justified when You speak and blameless when You judge. (NASB)

Any parent knows the difference between a genuine apology and a get-off-the-hook apology—a quick "sorry, sorry" as the child runs off down the hall. What Isaiah experienced was true conviction and repentance, the contrite and broken heart of one who knows he or she has done wrong and has insulted the one true and living God. Yet I fear that so much of what we think is confession is not confession at all. It is merely a hasty half apology, not the kind of brokenness we see in Psalm 51 or Isaiah 6. We must be brought face-to-face with our sin.

WHERE AUTHENTIC WORSHIP LEADS: PROCLAMATION OF THE GOSPEL

Third, authentic worship will lead to a display of redemption, by which I mean the proclamation of the gospel. What we see in Isaiah 6:6–7 is a display of redemption: "Then one of the seraphim flew to me, having in his hand a burning coal that he had taken with tongs from the altar. And he touched my mouth and said: 'Behold, this has touched your lips; your guilt is taken away, and your sin atoned for.'"

This scene is clearly an anticipation of the work of Christ. It is a unilateral act of God, a unilateral propitiatory sacrifice. It is a picture of atonement. Isaiah brought absolutely nothing to God. He had been brought face-to-face with his sin, and he now realizes that redemption is all of grace, and that it is costly. The coal, after all, came from the altar of sacrifice, not from a campfire.

> Turning to God through confession, we experience the display and declaration of redemption.

Martin Luther said that Isaiah saw himself first as he truly is—a sinner who was undone—and next as one who knows redemption. Luther states, "But it turned out for the salvation of the prophet that he was thus thrust down to hell, so that he might be led away and lead others away from that uncleanness of the Law to the purity of Christ, so that he alone might reign. Here now a resurrection from the dead takes place."[8] That must happen in our worship as well. True worship requires seeing the true and living God, and then seeing ourselves as we actually are in our sinfulness. Turning to God through confession, we experience the display and declaration of redemption.

True worship always proclaims the gospel, the good news of what God has done in Jesus Christ. It proclaims the work of Christ, and it centers in the cross. With the apostle Paul we say, "In the cross of Christ we glory." We proclaim liberty to the captive, and grace and pardon to all who believe in His name.

WHAT AUTHENTIC WORSHIP REQUIRES:
A RESPONSE

Fourth, given what God has done, authentic worship requires a response. Isaiah recounts, "Then I heard the voice of the Lord, saying, 'Whom shall I send, and who will go for Us?' Then I said, 'Here am I! Send me!'" (v. 8 NASB). We see in this passage a sending out similar to that in Matthew 28:18–20, when the Lord commanded His disciples, "All authority in heaven and on earth has been given to me. Go therefore . . ." Those disciples were to go and make disciples of all the nations, baptizing them in the name of the Father, and the Son, and the Holy Spirit, teaching them to observe all that He commanded them. Worship calls for an ongoing response seen in the proclamation of the gospel in personal evangelism and in missions. If our worship is weakened, our missionary witness will be weakened as well. We will forget the God who has sent us, and we will neglect the content of the message of redemption with which He has sent us.

One recent writer on worship has commented, "It is not *how* you worship. It's *who* you worship." I would argue that the *who* determines the *how*. Perhaps that is why so many churches have rejected, or at least neglected, the central component of Christian worship—the preaching of the Word. I realize it might seem bold—and maybe even shocking to some—to say that preaching is the central component of Christian worship. But how could it be otherwise? For it is primarily through the preaching of Scripture that we come to a true vision of the living God, recognize our own sinfulness, hear the declaration of redemption, and are called to a response of faith, repentance, and service.

Despite all that, most outside observers would probably guess that it is music that stands at the center of our worship. The fact is music now fills the empty space in most evangelical worship and provides most of the energy in the worship service. Intense planning, financial resources, and preparation are invested in the musical dimensions of worship. Professional staff and an army of volunteers spend much of the week in rehearsals and practice sessions, as many evangelical churches seem intensely concerned to replicate studio-quality musical presentations. All this is not lost on the congregation. Some Christians actually "shop churches" in order to find one that offers a worship style and experience that fits their expectation. In most communities, churches are known for their worship styles and musical programs. Those dissatisfied with what they find at one church can quickly move to another, sometimes using the language of self-expression to explain that the new church "meets our needs" or "allows us to worship."

> The heart of Christian worship is the authentic preaching of the Word of God.

A concern for true biblical worship was at the very heart of the Reformation. But even Martin Luther, who wrote hymns and required his preachers to be trained in song, would not recognize this modern preoccupation with music as legitimate or healthy. Why? *Because the Reformers were convinced that the heart of true biblical worship was the preaching of the Word of God.*

Music is one of God's most precious gifts to His people, and it is a language by which we may worship God in spirit and in truth. The hymns of the faith convey rich confessional and theological content, and many modern choruses recover a sense of doxology formerly lost in many evangelical churches. But music is not the central act of Christian worship—nor is evangelism, nor even the ordinances. The heart of Christian worship is the authentic preaching of the Word of God.

This centrality of preaching is seen in both testaments of Scripture. It was the apostle Paul, for example, who told Timothy in no uncertain terms, "I charge you therefore before God and the Lord Jesus Christ, who will judge the living and the dead at His appearing and His kingdom, Preach the Word!" In Nehemiah 8, as we will see in more detail in the next chapter, we find a remarkable portrait of expository preaching, when the people demand that Ezra the scribe bring the book of the law to the assembly. Ezra stands

> In far too many churches, the Bible is nearly silent.

on a raised platform and reads from the book of the law, "translating to give the sense so that they understood the reading" (Nehemiah 8:8 NASB). When he opens the book to read, the assembly rises to its feet in honor of the Word of God, and their response to the reading is to answer, "Amen, Amen!"

This text is a sobering indictment of much contemporary Christianity. According to the text, a demand for biblical preaching erupted within the hearts of the people. They gathered as a congregation and summoned the preacher. This reflects an intense hunger and thirst for the preaching of the Word of God. Where is this desire evident among today's evangelicals? Moreover, where is the faithfulness of preachers to confront their people with the preached Word of God? There seems to be a sense that people will be more affected by the gospel if it is presented in a slickly produced multimedia production, or even if we dispense with preaching altogether in favor of a purely subjective and emotional worship "experience." Yet what was it that brought the Israelites to their God-honoring response of "Amen, Amen!"? It was the exposition of the Word. Ezra did not stage an event or orchestrate a spectacle. He simply and carefully proclaimed the Word of God.

In far too many churches, the Bible is nearly silent. The public reading of Scripture has been dropped from many services, and the sermon has been sidelined, reduced to a brief devotional appended to the music. Many preachers accept this as a necessary concession to the age of entertainment, and are thus left with the modest hope of including a brief message of encouragement or exhortation before the conclusion of the service.

Michael Green pointedly put the problem like this: "This is the age of the sermonette, and sermonettes make Christianettes."[9] The anemia of evangelical worship—all the music and energy aside—is directly attributable to the absence of genuine expository preaching. If we as pastors are truly serious about giving our people a true vision of God, showing them their own sinfulness, proclaiming to them the gospel of Jesus Christ, and encouraging them to obedient service in response to that gospel, then we will devote our lives to preaching the Word. That is our task and our calling—to confront our congregations with nothing less than the living and active Word of God, and to pray that the Holy Spirit will thereby open eyes, convict consciences, and apply that Word to human hearts.

CHAPTER 2

THE GROUND OF PREACHING
Our Triune God

"Preach the Word!" That simple imperative frames the act of preaching as an act of obedience, and that is where any theology of preaching must begin. Preaching did not emerge from the church's experimentation with communication techniques. The church does not preach because preaching is thought to be a good idea or an effective technique. The sermon has not earned its place in Christian worship by proving its utility in comparison with other means of communication or aspects of worship. Rather, we preach because we have been commanded to preach.

Preaching is a commission—a charge. As Paul stated boldly, it is the task of the minister of the gospel to "preach the word . . . in season and out of season" (2 Timothy 4:2). A theology of preaching begins with the humble acknowledgment that preaching is not a human invention but a gracious creation of God and a central part of His revealed will for the church.

Thus preaching is communication, but it is not *mere* communication. It is human speech, but it is also much more than speech. As Ian Pitt-Watson noted, preaching is not even "a kind of speech communication that happens to be about God." Its ground, its goal, and its glory are all located in the sovereign will of God. Preaching is therefore an inescapably theological act, for the preacher dares to speak of God and, in a very real sense, for God. For that reason, a theology of preaching should take Trinitarian form, reflecting the very nature of the self-revealing God. In so doing, it bears witness to the God who speaks, the Son who saves, and the Spirit who illuminates.

> **God has spoken, and He has commanded us to speak of Him.**

THE GOD WHO SPEAKS

True preaching begins with this confession: We preach because God has spoken. That fundamental conviction is the fulcrum of the Christian faith and of Christian preaching. The Creator of the universe, the omniscient, omnipotent, omnipresent Lord, chose of His own sovereign will to reveal Himself to us. Supreme and complete in His holiness, needing nothing and hidden from our view, God condescended to speak to us and even to reveal Himself to us. As Carl F. H. Henry suggests, revelation is "a divinely initiated activity, God's free communication by which he alone turns his personal privacy into a deliberate disclosure of his reality."[1] In an act of holy graciousness, God gave up His comprehensive privacy that we might know Him. God's revelation is the radical ground upon which we dare to speak of God.

Our God-talk must therefore begin and end with what God has said concerning Himself. Preaching is not the business of speculating about God's nature, will, or ways, but is bearing witness to what God has spoken concerning Himself. Preaching does not consist of speculation but of exposition. The preacher dares to speak the Word of truth to a generation that rejects the very notion of objective, public truth. This is not rooted in the preacher's arrogant claim to have discovered worldly wisdom or to have penetrated the secrets of the universe. To the contrary, the preacher dares to proclaim truth on the basis of God's sovereign self-disclosure. God has spoken, and He has commanded us to speak of Him.

The Bible bears witness to itself as the written Word of God, a claim that springs from the fact that God has spoken. In the Old Testament alone, the phrases "the Lord said," "the Lord spoke," and "the word of the Lord came" appear at least 3,808 times. This confession brings the preacher face-to-face with Scripture as divine revelation, for the authority of Scripture is none other than the authority of God Himself. As the Reformation formula testifies, "where Scripture speaks, God speaks."

> Speaking on the basis of what God has spoken is both arduous and glorious.

God has called the church to speak of Him on the basis of His Word and deeds, and therefore all Christian preaching is biblical preaching. In fact, that formula is axiomatic. Those who preach from some other authority or text may speak with great effect and attractiveness, but they are preaching "another gospel," and their words will betray them. Christian preaching is not an easy task. Those who are called to preach bear a heavy duty. As Martin Luther confessed, "If I could come down with a good conscience, I would rather be stretched out on a wheel and carry stones than preach one sermon." Speaking on the basis of what God has spoken is both arduous and glorious.

A theology of preaching must begin with the confession that the God who speaks has the ultimate claim upon us. He who spoke a word and brought a world into being created us from the dust. What a wonderful and humbling thought to realize that God has chosen enlivened dust like us to bear testimony to His glory.

Let's be honest: The act of preaching would smack of unmitigated arrogance and overreaching were it not for the fact that it is God Himself who has given us the task. In that light, preaching is not an act of arrogance at all but rather of humility. True preaching is never an exhibition of the brilliance or intellect of the preacher but an exposition of the wisdom and power of God.

This kind of humility in preaching is possible only when the preacher stands in submission to the text of Scripture. Finally, it is simply a matter of authority. Either the preacher himself or the text will determine what is said. As preachers of God's Word, we dare not confuse our own authority with that of the biblical text. To do so would be an act of unmitigated arrogance. We are called not only to *preach* but to preach *the Word*.

John Calvin understood this truth when he affirmed that "the Word goeth out of the mouth of God in such a manner that it likewise goeth out of the mouth of men; for God does not speak openly from heaven, but employs men as His instruments."[2] Calvin understood that preaching is to be the process by which God uses human instruments to speak what He Himself has spoken. God uses preachers, Calvin offered, "rather than to thunder at us and drive us away." Thus, "it is a singular privilege that He deigns to consecrate to Himself the mouths and toungues [sic] of men in order that His voice may resound in them."[3]

All Christian preaching springs from the truth that God has spoken in word and deed, and that He has chosen human vessels to bear witness to Himself and His gospel. We speak because we cannot be silent. We speak because God has spoken.

THE SON WHO SAVES

"In the past," wrote the author of Hebrews, "God spoke to our forefathers through the prophets at many times and in various ways, but in these last days he has spoken to us by his Son, whom he appointed heir of all things, and through whom he made the universe"

(Hebrews 1:1–2 NIV). The God who reveals Himself (*Deus Revelatus*) has spoken supremely and definitively through His Son.

Carl Henry once stated that only a theology based in a vision of "divine invasion" could lay claim upon the church. The same holds true for a theology of preaching. All Christian preaching is unabashedly christological. Christian preaching points to the incarnation of God in Christ as the stack pole of truth and the core of Christian confession. "God was in Christ reconciling the world to Himself," Paul said (2 Corinthians 5:19 NASB). Thus, preaching is itself an act of grace. It is the primary means by which the redeemed make clear God's initiative toward us in Christ and bear witness to the Son who saves. That message of divine salvation, the unmerited act of God in Christ, is the criterion by which all preaching is to be judged.

> The cross is simultaneously the most divisive and the most unifying event in human history.

If preaching takes its ground and derives its power from God's revelation in the Son, then the cross is the paramount symbol and event of Christian proclamation. "We do not preach ourselves," pressed Paul, "but Jesus Christ as Lord" (2 Corinthians 4:5 NIV). When Paul preached, his message was centered on the cross as the definitive criterion of preaching. He understood that the cross is simultaneously the most divisive and the most unifying event in human history. The message of the gospel does not end with the cross, however. It continues to the empty tomb. All Christian preaching includes the proclamation of the resurrection, which means that to preach the message of the Son who saves is to spread the world's most hopeful message.

A theology of preaching includes both a "theology of the cross" and a "theology of glory." The cross brings the eclipse of all human pretensions and enlightenment, but the empty tomb reveals the radiant sunrise of God's personal glory. If Christ has not been raised, asserted Paul, "our preaching is useless" (1 Corinthians 15:14 NIV). This glimpse of God's glory does not afford the church or the preacher a sense of triumphalism or self-sufficiency. To the contrary, it points to the sufficiency of God and to the glory only He enjoys—a glory He has shared with us in the person and work of Jesus Christ. The reflection of that revelation is the radiance and glory of preaching.

Even so, Paul was under no illusion that his message would be enthusiastically received. He knew that what he preached would be called foolishness (1 Corinthians 1:18). Any honest and faithful theology of preaching must acknowledge that charges of foolishness are not incidental to the homiletical task. They are central, and every Christian preacher should be prepared for them. Most of the world will be frustrated with what we preach, for the cross abolishes human self-sufficiency and worldly wisdom. Christian preachers will always labor under the temptation to preach a message that will be acclaimed by the world as learned, wise, and erudite. To aim for that kind of worldly applause, however, is to empty the cross of its power (see 1 Corinthians 1:17).

Both the preacher and the hearers are dependent upon the work of the Holy Spirit for any adequate understanding of the text.

Writing to the church at Corinth, Paul explained: "My message and my preaching were not with wise and persuasive words, but with a demonstration of the Spirit's power, so that your faith might not rest on men's wisdom, but on God's power" (1 Corinthians 2:4–5 NIV). To preach the gospel of the Son who saves is to reject any notion that it is communication technique or human persuasion that is the measure of homiletical effectiveness. As James Denney stated so plainly, "No man can give at once the impression that he himself is clever and that Christ is mighty to save."[4] Our aim in preaching is to be faithful to the gospel of Jesus Christ. The effect of that gospel on human hearts, we leave in the hands of God and His Holy Spirit.

THE SPIRIT WHO ILLUMINATES

The preacher stands before the congregation as the external minister of the Word, but it is the Holy Spirit who works as the internal minister of that same Word. A biblical theology of preaching must take the role of the Spirit into full view, for without an understanding of the work of the Spirit, the task of preaching is robbed of its balance and power.

The neglect of the work of the Holy Spirit is a symptom of the decline of biblical Trinitarianism that marks our age. Spurgeon warned, "You might as well expect to raise the dead by whispering in their ears, as hope to save souls by preaching to them, if it were not for the agency of the Holy Spirit."[5] The Spirit performs His work of inspiration, indwelling, regeneration, and sanctification as the inner minister of the Word; it is the Spirit's ministry of illumination that allows the Word of the Lord to break forth. The Reformation saw a new acknowledgment of this truth, the union of Word and Spirit. And this Trinitarian doctrine produced preaching that was both bold and humble—bold in its content, but spoken by humble humans who knew their utter dependence upon God.

Both the preacher and the hearers are dependent upon the work of the Holy Spirit for any adequate understanding of the text. As Calvin warned, "No one should now hesitate to confess that he is able to understand God's mysteries only in so far as he is illumined by God's grace. He who attributes any more understanding to himself is all the more blind because he does not recognize his own blindness."[6] This has been the confession of great preachers from the first century to the present, and the absence of a conscious dependence upon the Holy Spirit is a sign that the preacher does not understand his task and calling. Tertullian, for example, called the Spirit his "Vicar" who ministered the Word to himself and to his congregation.

For the hearers of God's Word, the role of the Holy Spirit is no less crucial. For it is only by the inner testimony of the Spirit that they come truly to understand. Calvin described this internal testimony of the Holy Spirit as being absolutely necessary in order for the individual to receive the Word:

> For as God alone is a fit witness of himself in His Word, so also the Word will not find acceptance in men's hearts before it is sealed by the inward testimony of the Spirit. The same Spirit, therefore, who has spoken through the mouths of the prophets must penetrate into our hearts to persuade us that they faithfully proclaimed what had been divinely commanded.[7]

Martin Luther affirmed this same truth in various ways, most famously in his exhortation to his young students that they must preach the Word faithfully in order to get the Word to the ears of the congregation. After that, Luther insisted, only the Holy Spirit could take the Word from the ear into the human heart.

Luther had another important point to make as well. Even as the preacher is dependent upon the work of the Holy Spirit in the preaching of the Word, Luther insisted, the Father had willed that the Spirit should work uniquely through the Word and not independent of it. He rejected the notion that the Holy Spirit would impart spiritual life through sacraments or other actions apart from the Word. In Luther's own words:

> Therefore no one desiring comfort should wait until the Holy Spirit presents Christ to him personally or speaks to him directly from heaven. He gives His testimony publicly, in the sermon. There you must seek Him and wait for Him until He touches your heart through the Word that you hear with your ears, and thus He also testifies of Christ inwardly through His working.[8]

This kind of confidence in the Holy Spirit's work through the Word—and *only* through the Word—would be a much-needed corrective for today's confused church.

The same God who called forth human vessels and set them to preach also promised the power of the Spirit. Martyn Lloyd-Jones was aware that preachers often forget this promise:

> Seek Him always. But go beyond seeking Him; expect Him. Do you expect anything to happen when you get up to preach in a pulpit? Or do you just say to yourself, "Well, I have prepared my address, I am going to give them this address; some of them will appreciate it and some will not"? Are you expecting it to be the turning point in someone's life . . . ? That is what preaching is meant to do. . . . Seek this power, expect this power, yearn for this power; and when the power comes, yield to Him.[9]

To preach "in the Spirit" is to preach with the acknowledgment that the human instrument has no control over the message—and no control over the Word as it is set loose within the congregation. The Spirit, as John declared, testifies, "because the Spirit is the truth" (1 John 5:6).

THE GROUND, THE GOAL, AND THE GLORY OF PREACHING

J. I. Packer once defined preaching as "the event of God bringing to an audience a Bible-based, Christ-related, life-impacting message of instruction and direction from Himself through the words of a spokesperson."[10] That rather comprehensive definition depicts the process of God speaking forth His Word, using human instruments to proclaim His message, and then calling men and women unto Himself. If we are honest with ourselves, we must admit that preaching is a deadly business. As Spurgeon confirmed, "Life, death, hell, and worlds unknown may hang on the preaching and hearing of a sermon."

The preacher is a commissioned agent whose task is to speak because God has spoken, because the preacher has been entrusted with the telling of the gospel of the Son who saves, and because God has promised the power of the Spirit as the seal and efficacy of the preacher's calling. The ground of the preaching is none other than the revelation that God has addressed to us in Scripture. The goal of preaching is no more and no less than faithfulness to this calling. The glory of preaching is that God has promised to use preachers and preaching to accomplish His purpose and bring glory unto Himself.

Ultimately, a theology of preaching is essentially doxology. The ultimate purpose of the sermon is to glorify God and to reveal a glimpse of His glory to His creation. That God would choose such a means to express His own glory is beyond our understanding; it is rooted in the mystery of the will and wisdom of God.

CHAPTER 3

PREACHING IS EXPOSITORY

A Theology of Exposition

The preaching of the Word is central, irreducible, and nonnegotiable to authentic worship that pleases God. John Stott's simple declaration states the issue boldly: "Preaching is indispensable to Christianity."

More specifically, preaching is indispensable to Christian worship. But if preaching is central to Christian worship, what kind of preaching are we talking about? Certainly not the sermonettes described by Michael Green. The sheer weightlessness of much contemporary preaching is a severe indictment of our superficial Christianity. When the pulpit ministry lacks substance, the church is severed from the Word of God, and its health and faithfulness are immediately diminished.

I want to argue that the preaching that is central to Christian worship is expository preaching. In fact, *I believe that the only form of authentic Christian preaching is expository preaching.*

A CRISIS IN PREACHING

One of the hallmarks of our time is that we face a crisis of preaching. Indeed it would be an exercise in self-delusion if we tried to pretend that nothing is wrong with the preaching that happens in most evangelical churches. Let me ask some honest and difficult questions: If you picked an evangelical church at random and attended a Sunday morning service there, how likely is it that you would hear a faithful expository sermon, one that takes its message and its structure from the biblical text? If you answer that question honestly, you'll admit that your expectation would not be very high. Further, do you believe that as time passes it is becoming more likely or less likely that you would hear an expository message in that random church?

I am convinced that we add to the confusion by discussing expository preaching as merely one *kind* of preaching—or even the *best* kind. When we fall into that pattern, we do serious injury to the scriptural vision of preaching. Let's be clear. According to the Bible, exposition is preaching. And preaching is exposition.

Here we must deal not only with what preaching really is but also with what it is not. Much of what happens in pulpits across America today is not preaching, even though the preacher—and probably his congregation along with him—would claim that it is. Preaching is not the task of saying something interesting about God, nor is it delivering a religious discourse or narrating a story.

Many evangelicals are seduced by the proponents of topical and narrative preaching. The declarative force of Scripture is blunted by a demand for story, and the textual shape of the Bible is supplanted by topical considerations. In many pulpits, the Bible, if referenced at all, becomes merely a source for pithy aphorisms or convenient narratives. Moreover, the therapeutic concerns of the culture too often set the agenda for evangelical preaching. Issues of the self predominate, and the congregation expects to hear simple answers to complex problems. The essence of most therapeutic preaching comes down to an affirmation of the self and its importance. Evangelicals, much like their secular neighbors, now represent the age of "psychological man" so well described by Philip Reiff. The "triumph of the therapeutic" hits very close to home when evangelicals are honest about the preaching they want to hear and expect to receive.

Furthermore, postmodernism claims intellectual primacy in the culture, and even if they do not surrender entirely to doctrinal relativism, Americans allow and demand moral autonomy and a minimum of intellectual and moral requirements. The average congregant expects to make his or her own final decisions about all the important issues of life, from worldview to lifestyle.

However, the solid truth of Christianity stands in stark contrast to these flimsy pretensions of postmodernity. As theologian David F. Wells notes, "Sustaining orthodoxy and framing Christian belief in doctrinal terms requires habits of reflection and judgment that are simply out of place in our culture and increasingly are disappearing from evangelicalism as well."[1] Consequently, the appetite for serious preaching has virtually disappeared among many Christians, who are content to have their fascinations with themselves encouraged from the pulpit.

One symptom of our modern confusion is found in the fact that so many preachers would claim that their preaching is expository,

> The heart and soul of expository preaching . . . is reading the Word of God and then explaining it to the people so that they understand it.

even though this often means no more than that the preacher has a biblical text in mind, no matter how tenuous may be the actual relationship between the text and the sermon. One of the first steps to a recovery of authentic Christian preaching is to stop saying, "I prefer expository preaching." Rather, we should define exactly what we mean when we say "preach." What we mean is, very simply, reading the text and explaining it—reproving, rebuking, exhorting, and patiently teaching directly from the text of Scripture. If you are not doing that, then you are not preaching.

No better portrait of expository preaching could be found than that in Nehemiah 8:8. After the people gather at the Water Gate and demand that "the book" be brought forward, the text says of Ezra and his fellow scribes that "they read from the book, from the law of God, clearly, and they gave the sense, so that the people understood the reading." "Giving the sense" is not merely the act of translating from one language to another. It has to do with explaining a text, breaking it down, and making its meaning clear to the congregation. Essentially, this is what it means to preach. The heart and soul of expository preaching—of any true Christian preaching—is reading the Word of God and then explaining it to the people so that they understand it.

DEUTERONOMY 4 AND EXPOSITORY PREACHING

If we are to recover authentic preaching of God's Word, one of the most important tasks facing us is to articulate a theology of expository preaching. Deuteronomy 4 is a good place to begin, for it is there that God speaks to His people and reminds them what it is that makes them unique among the peoples of the earth. What He says has direct relevance to expository preaching.

> For ask now of the days that are past, which were before you, since the day that God created man on the earth, and ask from one end of heaven to the other, whether such a great thing as this has ever happened or was ever heard of. Did any people ever hear the voice

of a god speaking out of the midst of the fire, as you have heard, and still live? Or has any god ever attempted to go and take a nation for himself from the midst of another nation, by trials, by signs, by wonders, and by war, by a mighty hand and an outstretched arm, and by great deeds of terror, all of which the Lord your God did for you in Egypt before your eyes? To you it was shown, that you might know that the Lord is God; there is no other besides him. Out of heaven he let you hear his voice, that he might discipline you. And on earth he let you see his great fire, and you heard his words out of the midst of the fire. And because he loved your fathers and chose their offspring after them and brought you out of Egypt with his own presence, by his great power, driving out before you nations greater and mightier than yourselves, to bring you in, to give you their land for an inheritance, as it is this day, know therefore today, and lay it to your heart, that the Lord is God in heaven above and on the earth beneath; there is no other. Therefore you shall keep his statutes and his commandments, which I command you today, that it may go well with you and with your children after you, and that you may prolong your days in the land that the Lord your God is giving you for all time.

—DEUTERONOMY 4:32–40

The historical setting of this passage is very important. The children of Israel are in the wilderness, and Moses is preparing them to enter the land of promise. Behind them is the entire history of the exodus from Egypt and the forty years of wandering in the desert— the giving of the law at Sinai and Horeb, and the rebellion at Kadesh-barnea. They stood now on the bank of the Jordan River, and on the other side was the Promised Land.

In the great sermons that comprise the book of Deuteronomy, the Lord is speaking to His people through Moses, so that they would be prepared for the challenge that lay before them. The book is called *Deutero-nomos* because it is a second giving of the law. As Moses lays the Lord's commands before the people yet again, they have another opportunity to be faithful rather than faithless, obedient rather than disobedient when they face their enemies in the land of promise. Would they be ready?

Notice that even as it is a book of preparation, the book of Deuteronomy is not primarily a military briefing. It is not primarily about demographics and geography. Above all, it is about the Word of God. It is about the fact that God has spoken, and His people need to be ready to hear Him and obey. The intensity here is enormous, because the necessity of obedience is a matter of survival for Israel. You see, the entire theology of Deuteronomy comes down to the fact that God has spoken. Thus hearing and obeying is life, but refusing to hear and disobeying is death. Moses wants the people of Israel to know that life and death hang in the balance of their willingness to hear God's Word and respond to it. It is a matter of life or death.

I believe that the central problem in our crisis of preaching today is that somehow we believe this has changed. We no longer believe that hearing and responding to the Word of God is a matter of crucial importance. That is the only plausible reason I can offer for why expositional preaching is in decline, or even absent, in so many pulpits. Before the decline in expository preaching, there was the abandonment of the conviction that the Word of God comes as a matter of life and death.

DEVELOPING A PASSION FOR EXPOSITORY PREACHING

The situation, however, is not irrecoverable—not if we regain a conviction that our spiritual lives and the life of the church itself depend on hearing and responding to the Word of God in Scripture. Let's consider three things that we learn from Deuteronomy 4, three points that can help us to develop both a theology of and a passion for expository preaching.

First, the only true and living God is the God who speaks.

We know who God is not because any of us was smart enough to figure Him out, but because out of His own love, grace, and mercy He has spoken to us. Moses says this explicitly in Deuteronomy 4:32: "To you it was shown, that you might know that the Lord is God; there is no other besides him." The Israelites would not have known God at all unless He had spoken to them. This is the miracle of revelation, and I fear that we give this doctrine inadequate attention in our churches through our teaching and preaching. Instead of recognizing God's speaking to us in Scripture as a miracle of grace, we treat it as of little account. Instead of preaching the Word of God, we preach pop psychology and culture, or we tell compelling stories.

In Deuteronomy 4:10–19, Moses makes clear to the people of Israel that their very lives depended on hearing and obeying God's Word:

> On the day that you stood before the Lord your God at Horeb, the Lord said to me, "Gather the people to me, that I may let them hear my words, so that they may learn to fear me all the days that they live on the earth, and that they may teach their children so." And you came near and stood at the foot of the mountain, while the mountain burned with fire to the heart of heaven, wrapped in darkness, cloud, and gloom. Then the Lord spoke to you out of the midst of the fire. You heard the sound of words, but saw no form; there was only a voice. And he declared to you his covenant, which he commanded you to perform, that is, the Ten Commandments, and he wrote them on two tablets of stone. And the Lord commanded me at that time to teach you statutes and rules, that you might do them in the land that you are going over to possess.
>
> Therefore watch yourselves very carefully. Since you saw no form on the day that the Lord spoke to you at Horeb out of the midst of the fire, beware lest you act corruptly by making a carved image for yourselves, in the form of any figure, the likeness of male or female, the likeness of any animal that is on the earth, the likeness of any winged bird that flies in the air, the likeness of anything that creeps on the ground, the likeness of any fish that is in the water under the earth. And beware lest you raise your eyes to heaven, and when you

see the sun and the moon and the stars, all the host of heaven, you
be drawn away and bow down to them and serve them, things that
the Lord your God has allotted to all the peoples under the whole
heaven.

Notice how Moses lovingly reminds the people that *they were there*
when God spoke. "You came near," he says. "Do you remember how
you stood at the foot of the mountain? Do you remember when you
heard the voice of God speaking from the midst of the fire? You heard
God's voice!"

Then more pointedly in verse 15, he says, "You saw no form."
You didn't see God. You heard Him. That was very different from the
pagan idols that surrounded Israel, and it showed them that their God
was the only true and living God. The pagans could see their idols.
They could even speak to them. But the pagans' idols never spoke.
They were silent. You see, that's the grand distinction made in the
Old Testament over and over again between the true God and the
false idols. The pagan peoples see their gods and speak to their gods,
but the one true and living God is never seen, and yet He speaks to
His people.

Elijah used this when he confronted the pagan priests at Mount
Carmel. First Kings 18:26–29 recounts the story:

And they took the bull that was given them, and they prepared it
and called upon the name of Baal from morning until noon, saying,
"O Baal, answer us!" But there was no voice, and no one answered.
And they limped around the altar that they had made. And at noon
Elijah mocked them, saying, "Cry aloud, for he is a god. Either he is
musing, or he is relieving himself, or he is on a journey, or perhaps he
is asleep and must be awakened." And they cried aloud and cut
themselves after their custom with swords and lances, until the blood
gushed out upon them. And as midday passed, they raved on until
the time of the offering of the oblation, but there was no voice. No
one answered; no one paid attention.

What a haunting passage. Despite all the frantic dancing and blood-letting, "there was no voice and no one answered" (verse 26). In response to all the raving by those pagan priests, "no one answered; no one paid attention" (verse 29).

Jeremiah similarly says of the pagan idols, "Their idols are like scarecrows in a cucumber field, and they cannot speak" (Jeremiah 10:5). And Paul tells his readers in 1 Corinthians 12:2, "You know that when you were pagans you were led astray to mute idols, however you were led." Throughout Scripture, the contrast is pressed between the mute, dumb idols that sit there like scarecrows in a cucumber field, and the one, living, *speaking* God.

Many evangelicals today believe that God *spoke,* but doubt whether He *speaks.*

This reminds us again of the gift of revelation, God's forfeiting of His own personal privacy, as Carl Henry put it. Stop and think about that. The God who needs nothing, sovereign in His majesty and infinite in His perfections, decided to reveal Himself to us so we might know Him. If that is true, then wouldn't you think that a people who are the recipients of such a gift would live by it, hunger for it, and cling to it?

I fear that there are many evangelicals today who believe that God *spoke* but doubt whether He *speaks.* They know and talk about the fact that God spoke in the Old Testament but think now that He no longer does so and that they must therefore invent new ways to convince people to love Him. But if you call yourself a preacher of God's Word, and you think that all of God's speaking was in the past, then resign. I say that with deadly seriousness. If you do not believe that God now speaks from His Word—the Bible—then what are you doing every Sunday morning? If you are not confident that God speaks as you rightly read and explain the Word of God, then you should quit.

But if you do believe that—if you truly believe that God speaks through His Word—then why would you substitute *anything else* in place of the expository preaching of the Bible? What is more important for your people than to hear from God, and how else is that going to happen unless you, like Ezra, open the book, read it, and explain it to them? Just as in Deuteronomy, this is a matter of life and death, and far too many pastors who deeply believe that God does speak have abandoned His voice in Scripture.

Second, God's true people are those who hear God speaking to them.

Time and time again in Deuteronomy, Moses says to the people, "Remember who you are! You are the people to whom Yahweh spoke, the people who received the Word of God at Horeb. He did not speak to everyone, *only* to you!" The point here is that the doctrine of revelation is directly tied to the doctrine of election. How do we know who God's people are? God's people are those to whom He speaks. The fact is, God did not speak to all the nations of the earth. He spoke to Israel, and by that very fact they were identified as His chosen people.

By reminding the Israelites that God spoke to them alone, Moses was not trying to incite the Israelites to pride, arrogance, or self-confidence. On the contrary, he was telling them to humble themselves, realizing that it was only by grace and mercy that God chose to speak to Israel rather than to some other nation. "It was not because you were more in number than any other people that the Lord set his love on you and chose you," he tells them in Deuteronomy 7:7, "for you were the fewest of all peoples." Rather, God chose to speak to them simply "because the Lord loves you and is keeping the oath that he swore to your fathers" (Deuteronomy 7:8). Israel was indeed an elect, chosen, and blessed nation, but that status was all of God's grace.

That is exactly the thrust of the passage in Deuteronomy 4:32–40, where Moses asks Israel four questions that are intended to remind them of how greatly and specially they have been blessed. The first of those questions is in verse 32: "Indeed, ask now concerning the former days which were before you, since the day that God created man on the earth, and inquire from one end of the heavens to the other. Has anything been done like this great thing?" (NASB). The exodus, the crushing of Pharaoh's army, the giving of the law, the entirety of God's dealings with Israel—had anything like this ever happened before? The answer, of course, is no. Israel's experience with God was utterly unique, and that is how they could know that they were God's people.

At the end of verse 32 is the second question: "Or has anything been heard like it?" Was there even a rumor out there of another people saying that their god rescued them from slavery, spoke to them, and chose them for his own glory? No! Once again, Israel was alone in that experience.

A third question appears in verse 34: "Has any god ever attempted to go and take a nation for himself from the midst of another nation, by trials, by signs, by wonders, and by war, by a mighty hand and an outstretched arm, and by great deeds of terror, all of which the Lord your God did for you in Egypt before your eyes?" Among the nations of the world, Israel was a captive people, a nation of slaves. Yet their captivity was also the means by which God would make Himself known to them. By rescuing them from Egypt, indeed by *taking* them, as the text puts it, with His outstretched arm, the Lord showed both to the world and to the Israelites themselves that they were His chosen and special people.

The fourth question is found in verse 33 (NASB), and it is one of the sweetest and most powerful questions asked anywhere in Scripture: "Has any people heard the voice of God speaking from the midst of the fire, as you have heard it, and survived?" How does Israel know that it

> You know that you are a believer in the Lord Jesus Christ . . . because you have heard the Word of God, and you have believed it.

is God's people? How do they know that He has chosen them and them alone? It is because God spoke to them out of the fire, and they lived to tell about it. No other people on earth heard the voice of God speak from the fire. Only Israel, the chosen people of God.

The same idea is found in the New Testament too. In Matthew 13:11, Jesus says to His disciples, "To you it has been given to know the secrets of the kingdom of heaven, but to them it has not been given." That realization did not lead the disciples to arrogance. It was not "given" to them to understand because of any merit in them. The disciples were given the gift of understanding because, in His sovereign grace, God determined to glorify Himself in them. They could know they belonged to Jesus precisely because to them it had been "given to know the secrets of the kingdom of heaven." As Jesus tells them later, "Blessed are your eyes, for they see, and your ears, for they hear. Truly, I say to you, many prophets and righteous people longed to see what you see, and did not see it, and to hear what you hear, and did not hear it" (Matthew 13:16–17).

How do you know that you are a believer in the Lord Jesus Christ? How do you explain that? Quite simply, it is because you have heard the Word of God, and you have believed it. Throughout the New Testament, God's elect are called out and redeemed by means of hearing the Word of God. In John 5:24–25, for example, Jesus says,

> Truly, truly, I say to you, whoever hears my word and believes him who sent me has eternal life. He does not come into judgment, but has passed from death to life. Truly, truly, I say to you, an hour is coming, and is now here, when the dead will hear the voice of the Son of God, and those who hear will live.

The focus in that passage is on the *spiritually* dead (Jesus will talk about the rising of the *physically* dead a few verses later), and what brings these spiritually dead people to life is hearing the voice of the Son of God. Indeed it is only those who hear His Word and believe who pass from death to life and do not come into judgment.

The book of Acts also emphasizes over and over that it is the hearing of God's Word that the Holy Spirit uses to bring about saving faith.

In Acts 2:37, it is only after the people hear Peter's sermon that they cry out, "Brothers, what shall we do?" Acts 13:48 records that "when the Gentiles *heard this*, they began rejoicing and glorifying the word of the Lord, and as many as were appointed to eternal life believed." And Acts 16:14 records that the Lord "opened [Lydia's] heart to *pay attention* to what was *said* by Paul" (italics added).

Of course Paul makes this point most explicitly in Romans 10:13–14, where he writes: "For 'everyone who calls on the name of the Lord will be saved.' But how are they to call on him in whom they have not believed? And how are they to believe in him of whom they have never heard? And how are they to hear without someone preaching?"

God's elect people—those who will hear His voice and believe in Jesus Christ—are called out primarily by the preaching of the Word. Therefore to replace the expository preaching of God's Word with anything else at all is to abandon the means God has determined to use to call His people to Himself. Do you want to see the elect called out and redeemed under your ministry? Do you want to see sinners come to faith? Then your task really could not be clearer, for "Faith comes from hearing, and hearing from the word of Christ" (Romans 10:17).

Third, God's people depend for their very lives on hearing His Word.

For the Israelites, hearing God's Word and obeying it was a matter of life and death. "Therefore you shall keep his statutes and his commandments," Moses told them, "that it may go well with you and with your children after you, and that you may prolong your days in the land that the Lord your God is giving you for all time" (Deuteronomy 4:40). He makes the point again near the end of the book, in Deuteronomy 30:15–20.

> See, I have set before you today life and good, death and evil. If you obey the commandments of the Lord your God that I command you today, by loving the Lord your God, by walking in his ways, and by keeping his commandments and his statutes and his rules, then you

shall live and multiply, and the Lord your God will bless you in the land that you are entering to take possession of it. But if your heart turns away, and you will not hear, but are drawn away to worship other gods and serve them, I declare to you today, that you shall surely perish. You shall not live long in the land that you are going over the Jordan to enter and possess. I call heaven and earth to witness against you today, that I have set before you life and death, blessing and curse. Therefore choose life, that you and your offspring may live, loving the Lord your God, obeying his voice and holding fast to him, for he is your life and length of days, that you may dwell in the land that the Lord swore to your fathers, to Abraham, to Isaac, and to Jacob, to give them.

For Israel, God's Word was like the manna in the wilderness. They needed it every day, fresh and new, if they were to survive at all. To hear the Word and obey it was life for them. Not to hear and not to obey would result in death. So Israel lived by God's Word, and that Word became to them health, life, blessing, and even identity.

Read the Psalms, and you will see how Israel longed to hear and know God's Word. King David says in Psalm 19, for example,

> The law of the Lord is perfect, reviving the soul;
> the testimony of the Lord is sure, making wise the simple;
> the precepts of the Lord are right, rejoicing the heart;
> the commandment of the Lord is pure, enlightening the eyes;
> the fear of the Lord is clean, enduring forever;
> the rules of the Lord are true, and righteous altogether.
> More to be desired are they than gold, even much fine gold;
> sweeter also than honey and drippings of the honeycomb.
> Moreover, by them is your servant warned;
> In keeping them there is great reward.
> Let the words of my mouth and the meditation of my heart
>   be acceptable in your sight,
>   O Lord, my rock and my redeemer.
>
> —PSALM 19:7–11, 14

Psalm 119 similarly declares the psalmist's dependence on the Word of God. "If your law had not been my delight," he says, "I would have perished in my affliction. I will never forget your precepts, for by them you have given me life. I am yours; save me, for I have sought your precepts. The wicked lie in wait to destroy me, but I consider your testimonies" (verses 92–95). The people of Israel could not survive without the constant presence, knowledge, and hearing of God's Word.

The same is true in the New Testament. Paul gives this eloquent testimony in 2 Timothy 3:16–17: "All Scripture is breathed out by God and profitable for teaching, for reproof, for correction, and for training in righteousness, that the man of God may be competent, equipped for every good work."

> Preaching is therefore always a matter of life and death.

Scripture alone is breathed out by God, and thus it alone is profitable for these things. Nothing else in the world is. This is a testimony not only to the authority and perfection of Scripture but also to its sufficiency. It alone is sufficient for the teaching, reproof, correction, and training of God's people. As Christians, we live by the Word of God just as completely as Israel did. We know who God is only through the Scriptures, and we know who we are in Christ only through the Scriptures.

Preaching is therefore always a matter of life and death. The people in our churches depend for their very lives on the ministry of the Word; therefore our preaching had better be nothing less—and nothing *other*—than the exposition of the Bible. Nothing else will do. The question that faces us as preachers is not how we're going to grow our churches or inspire our people. It is not even how we can lead them to live more faithfully than they did before. The question that faces us is: Are these people going to live or are they going to die?

That's what was at stake in the Old Testament, and so it is also with Christian preaching. We have the Bible, and if we truly believe that Bible to be the written Word of God—the perfect, divinely inspired revelation of God—then expositional preaching is the only option available to us.

It all finally comes down to the question of who has the right to speak. Does the preacher have the right to speak, or does that right belong to God? That is the difference between life and death for our people. Do we think that God's elect will be called out by our own stories, gimmicks, and eloquence? Such thinking is arrogance. Can God's redeemed people live on our words alone? Will they be just fine if we don't read and explain God's Word to them? Obviously not. For life is found only in the Word of God.

In the end, our calling as preachers is really very simple. We study, we stand before our people, we read the text, and we explain it. We reprove, rebuke, exhort, encourage, and teach—and then we do it all again and again and again.

EXPOSITORY PREACHING
Its Definition and Characteristics

Let me offer a more formal definition of expository preaching as a framework for consideration:

Expository preaching is that mode of Christian preaching that takes as its central purpose the presentation and application of the text of the Bible. All other issues and concerns are subordinated to the central task of presenting the biblical text. As the Word of God, the text of Scripture has the right to establish both the substance and the structure of the sermon. Genuine exposition takes place when the preacher sets forth the meaning and message of the biblical text and makes clear how the Word of God establishes the identity and worldview of the church as the people of God.

Each part of this definition is important, and each part helps us to understand more fully how to follow Ezra's example in explaining the text of Scripture to our congregations.

EXPOSITORY PREACHING
AND THE WORD OF GOD

First, expository preaching is that mode of Christian preaching that takes as its central purpose the presentation and application of the text of the Bible. This means that expository preaching begins with the preacher's determination to present and explain the text of the Bible to his congregation. This simple starting point is a major issue of division in contemporary homiletics, for many preachers—from Harry Emerson Fosdick onward—assume that they must begin with a human problem or question and then work backward to the biblical text. On the contrary, expository preaching begins with the text and works from the text to apply its truth to the lives of believers. If this determination and commitment are not clear at the outset, something other than expository preaching will result.

Expository preaching is therefore inescapably bound to the serious work of exegesis. If the preacher is to explain the text, he must first study the text and devote the hours of study and research necessary to understand it. The pastor must invest the largest portion of his energy and intellectual engagement (not to mention his time) to this task of "accurately handling the word of truth" (2 Timothy 2:15 NASB). There are no shortcuts to genuine exposition. The expositor is not an explorer who returns to tell tales of the journey but a guide who leads the people into the text, teaching the arts of Bible study and interpretation even as he demonstrates the same.

The preacher rises in the pulpit to accomplish one central purpose—to set forth the message and meaning of the biblical text. This requires historical investigation, literary discernment, and the faithful employment of the *analogia fidei* ("analogy of faith"); i.e., interpreting Scripture by Scripture. It also requires the expositor to reject the modern conceit that what the text *meant* is not necessarily what it *means*. If the Bible is truly the enduring and eternal Word of God, it means what it meant even as it is newly applied in every generation.

Second, all other issues and concerns are subordinated to the central task of presenting the biblical text. Every preacher comes to the text and to the preaching event with a multitude of concerns and priorities in mind, many of which are undeniably legitimate and important in their own right. One of our aims in preaching, for example, is evangelism. We want to see people brought to faith in Christ through the preached Word. Another motive for our preaching is the edification of our people and their encouragement in the faith. All this takes place, however, only as we present and explain the biblical text itself. If a preacher leaves the pulpit without accomplishing that primary task, then no matter how much the congregation enjoyed the sermon or felt moved by it, his people will die.

If genuine exposition of the Word of God is to take place, then every other concern must be subordinate to the central and irreducible task of explaining and presenting the biblical text.

Third, the text of Scripture has the right to establish both the substance and the structure of the sermon. This is where many preachers will find themselves personally challenged in their own preaching. Because the Bible is the inerrant and infallible Word of God, the very shape of the biblical text is also divinely determined. God has spoken through the inspired human authors of Scripture, and each different genre of biblical literature—historical narrative, direct discourse, and apocalyptic symbolism, among others—demands that the preacher give careful attention to the structure of the text and allow it to shape the sermon. Far too many preachers come to the text with a sermonic shape in mind and a limited set of tools in hand. To be sure, the shape of the sermon may differ from preacher to preacher and should differ from text to text. But genuine exposition demands that the text establish the shape as well as the substance of the sermon.

Fourth, the preacher must make clear how the Word of God establishes the identity and worldview of the church as the people of God. Once the meaning of the text is set forth, the preacher moves to application. Applying biblical truth to the church's life is a necessary task of expository preaching. But application must follow the diligent and disciplined task of explaining the text itself. T. H. L. Parker, commenting on Calvin's homiletic method, describes preaching like this: "Expository preaching consists in the explanation and application of a passage of Scripture. Without explanation it is not expository; without application it is not preaching."[1]

Application is absolutely necessary, but it is also fraught with danger. Haddon Robinson describes the "heresy of application," warning that many preachers are faithful in the task of exegesis, but undermine the text at the point of application. At the other extreme are preachers who never get to the task of application at all, arguing that application is an attempt to do the work of the Holy Spirit. Certainly no preacher should ever believe that he can or should manipulate the human heart. But the faithful preacher understands the difference between the external application of the text to life and the Spirit's internal application of the Word to the heart. The preacher is responsible for setting forth the eternal words of Scripture. Only the Holy Spirit can apply those words to human hearts or even open eyes to understand and receive the text.

> The Bible determines reality for the church and stipulates a God-centered worldview.

In preaching the biblical text, the preacher explains how the Bible directs our thinking and living. This brings the task of expository preaching into direct confrontation with the postmodern worldview and the simple fact of human sinfulness. We do not want to be told how to think or how to live. Each of us desires to be the author of our own life script, the master of our own fate, our own judge and lawgiver and guide. But the Word of God lays a unique and privileged claim upon the church as the body of Christ. Every text demands a fundamental realignment of our basic worldview and way of life. As the Word of God, the biblical text has the right to establish our identity as the people of God and to determine our worldview. The Bible tells us who we are, locates us under the lordship of Jesus Christ, and establishes a worldview framed by the glory and sovereignty of God. Put simply, the Bible determines reality for the church and stipulates a God-centered worldview for the redeemed. Thus, the church is always mounting a counterrevolution to the spirit of the age, and preaching is the God-ordained means whereby the saints are armed and equipped for this battle and confrontation.

Furthermore, true exposition demands a hearing from God's people and presents all hearers with a decision. As John MacArthur explains, "I believe the goal of preaching is to compel people to make a decision. I want people who listen to me to understand exactly what God's Word demands of them when I am through. Then they must say either, 'Yes, I will do what God says,' or 'No, I won't do what God says.'"[2] Every sermon presents the hearer with a forced decision. We will either obey or disobey the Word of God. The sovereign authority of God operates through the preaching of His Word to demand obedience from His people.

> Authentic expository preaching will be marked by three distinct characteristics: authority, reverence, and centrality.

The preached Word, applied to the heart by the Holy Spirit, is the essential instrumentality through which God shapes His people. As the Reformers remind us, it is through preaching that Christ is present among His people.

MARKS OF AUTHENTIC EXPOSITORY PREACHING

When it is done rightly and faithfully, authentic expository preaching will be marked by three distinct characteristics: authority, reverence, and centrality. Expository preaching is authoritative. Moreover, it stands upon the very authority of the Bible as the Word of God. It requires and reinforces a sense of reverent expectation on the part of God's people. And finally, expository preaching demands the central place in Christian worship and is respected as the event through which the living God speaks to His people.

First, expository preaching is characterized by authority. Sociologist Richard Sennett of New York University notes that in times past a major anxiety of most persons was the loss of governing authority. Now the tables have been turned, and modern persons are anxious about any authority over them: "We have come to fear the influence of authority as a threat to our liberties, in the family and in society at large," Sennett writes. If previous generations feared the absence of authority, today we see "a fear of authority when it exists."[3]

The Enlightenment culture that gave birth to modernity was subversive of every form of authority, though it has taken some centuries for this rebellion against authority to work its way throughout society. In the postmodern culture of the West, authority is under attack in every form, and a sense of personal autonomy is basic to contemporary ideals of human rights and freedom. We will have no king to rule over us; no parent to discipline us; no teacher to instruct us; and no truth to bind us. As two recent observers lament, "Americans have embraced freedom so tightly, they can see only one aspect of it, the side of autonomy."[4]

Some homileticians suggest that preachers should simply embrace this new worldview and surrender any claim to an authoritative message. Those who have lost confidence in the authority of the Bible as the Word of God are left with little to say and no authority for their message. Fred Craddock, among the most influential figures in recent homiletic thought, famously describes today's preacher "as one without authority." His portrait of the preacher's predicament is haunting: "The old thunderbolts rust in the attic while the minister tries to lead his people through the morass of relativities and proximate possibilities."[5] "No longer can the preacher presuppose the general recognition of his authority as a clergyman, or the authority of his institution, or the authority of Scripture," Craddock argues. Summarizing the predicament of the postmodern preacher, he relates that the preacher "seriously asks himself whether he should continue to serve up monologue in a dialogical world."[6]

The obvious question to pose to Craddock's analysis is this: If we have no authoritative message, why preach? Without authority, the preacher and the congregation are involved in a massive waste of precious time. The very idea that preaching can be transformed into a dialogue between the pulpit and the pew indicates the confusion of our era.

Contrasted to this are the words of Martyn Lloyd-Jones: "Any study of church history, and particularly any study of the great periods of revival or reawakening, demonstrates above everything else just this one fact: that the Christian Church during all such periods has spoken with authority. The great characteristic of all revivals has been the authority of the preacher. There seemed to be something new, extra, and irresistible in what he declared on behalf of God."[7] In all true expository preaching, there is the note of authority. That is because the preacher dares to speak on behalf of God. He stands in the pulpit as a steward "of the mysteries of God" (1 Corinthians 4:1), declaring the truth of God's Word, proclaiming the power of that Word, and applying that Word to life. This is an admittedly audacious act. No one should even contemplate such an endeavor without absolute confidence in a divine call to preach and in the unblemished authority of the Scriptures.

The preaching ministry is not a profession to be joined but a call to be answered. The church has no need of religious functionaries preaching up-to-date messages based on the latest therapeutic remedy or philosophical fad. Charles Spurgeon instructed his student preachers to pay heed to their call: "We must feel that woe is unto us if we preach not the gospel; the word of God must be unto us as fire in our bones, otherwise if we undertake the ministry, we shall be unhappy in it, shall be unable to bear the self-denials incident to it, and shall be of little service to those among whom we minister."[8] Furthermore, the call to preach is not merely an existential experience or perception embraced by an individual, but a call that must be recognized and affirmed by the church. The teaching office is one of God's gifts to His people, not a career path for a "helping profession."

Standing on the authority of Scripture, the preacher declares a truth received, not a message invented.

The authority of the preacher is rooted in this divine call to preach, and the church must respect the preaching office. But in the final analysis, the ultimate authority for preaching is the authority of the Bible as the Word of God. Without this authority, the preacher stands naked and silent before the congregation and the watching world. If the Bible is not the Word of God, the preacher is involved in an act of self-delusion or professional pretension. Standing on the authority of Scripture, the preacher declares a truth received, not a message invented. The teaching office is not an advisory role based in religious expertise but a prophetic function whereby God speaks to His people.

The absence of authority in much contemporary preaching is directly attributable to the absence of confidence in the authority of the Bible. Once biblical authority is undermined and eroded, preaching becomes a pretense. The preacher stands to offer religious advice on the basis of the latest secular learning and the "spirituality" of the day. The dust of death covers thousands of pulpits across the land. But when the Bible's authority is recognized and honored, the pulpit stands as a summons to hear and obey the Word of God. True worship takes place when the authority of the Bible is rightly honored and the preaching of the Word is understood to be the event whereby God speaks to His people through His Word by the human instrumentality of His servants—the preachers.

Second, authentic expository preaching creates a sense of reverence among God's people. The congregation that gathered before Ezra and the other preachers demonstrated a love and reverence for the Word of God (Nehemiah 8). When the book was read, the people stood up, an act that reveals their sense of expectancy as the Word was read and preached.

Expository preaching both requires and eventually cultivates an attitude of reverence on the part of the congregation. Preaching is not a dialogue, but it does involve at least two parties—the preacher and the congregation. The congregation's role in the preaching event is to hear, receive, and obey the Word of God. In so doing, the church demonstrates reverence for the preaching and teaching of the Bible and understands that the sermon brings the Word of Christ near to the congregation. This is true worship.

Lacking reverence for the Word of God, many congregations are caught in a frantic quest for significance in worship. Christians leave worship services asking each other, "Did you get anything out of that?" Churches produce surveys to measure expectations for worship. Would you like more music? What kind? How about drama? Is our preacher sufficiently creative?

Expository preaching demands a very different set of questions. Will I obey the Word of God? How must my thinking be realigned by Scripture? How must I change my behavior to be fully obedient to the Word? These questions reveal submission to the authority of God and reverence for the Bible as His Word.

Likewise, the preacher must demonstrate his own reverence for God's Word by dealing truthfully and responsibly with the text. He must not be flippant or casual, much less dismissive or disrespectful. Of this we can be certain—no congregation will revere the Bible more than the preacher does.

Calvin instructed his congregation about authentic worship by reminding them of the purpose of preaching: "We come together in the name of the Lord. It is not to hear merry songs, to be fed with wind, that is, with a vain and unprofitable curiosity, but to receive spiritual nourishment. For God will have nothing preached in his name but that which will profit and edify."[9] Reverence is the only appropriate response to the acknowledgment that the Bible is the Word of God and that preaching is the proclamation of that Word to God's people. Luther continually pointed back to God as the divine author of the Word: "To be sure, I do hear the sermon; however, I am wont to ask, 'Who is speaking?' The pastor? By no means! You do not hear the pastor. Of course the voice is his, but the words he employs are really spoken by God. There I must hold the Word of God in high esteem that I may become an apt pupil of the Word. If we looked upon it as the Word of God, we would be glad to go to church, to listen to the sermon, and to pay attention to the precious Word."[10]

Third, expository preaching must be at the center of Christian worship. It is worth noting again: Worship properly directed to the honor and glory of God will find its center in the reading and preaching of the Word of God. Expository preaching cannot be assigned a supporting role in the act of worship. It must be central.

> God is most beautifully praised when His people hear His Word, love His Word, and obey His Word.

In the course of the Reformation, Luther's driving purpose was to restore preaching to its proper place in Christian worship. Referring to the incident between Mary and Martha in Luke 10, Luther reminded his congregation and students that Jesus Christ declared that "only one thing is necessary"—the preaching of the Word (Luke 10:42 NASB). Luther realized that the most important reform needed was to reestablish the reading and preaching of the Word as the central act of Christian worship.

That same reformation is needed in American evangelicalism today. Expository preaching must once again be central to the life of the church and central to Christian worship. In the end, the church will not be judged by its Lord for the quality of its music but for the faithfulness of its preaching. The preacher will be judged for his preaching, and the congregation will be judged for its hearing—and for the preaching it has demanded.

Hughes Oliphant Old's monumental study of preaching throughout the history of the church starts with the preaching of the biblical period. Looking at the preaching of the apostle Paul, Old gets to the heart of the matter:

> The preaching and the hearing of the Word of God is in the last analysis worship, worship in its most profound sense. Preaching is not an auxiliary activity to worship, nor is it some kind of preparation for worship which one hopes will follow. . . . The proclaiming of the Word of God, simply in itself, is high service to God. The solemn reading and preaching of Scripture in the midst of the congregation is a cultic act, if we may use that term, in continuity with the sacrifices of the Old Testament. Even more it fulfills these ancient cultic acts. The Old Testament sacrifices were the type, the foreshadow, of something far greater, the proclamation of the gospel. The reading and preaching of Scripture is worship of an even greater intensity, an even greater depth, and an even greater magnificence than were ever the sacrifices of the Temple.[11]

When today's evangelicals speak casually of the distinction between worship and preaching (meaning that the church will enjoy an offering of music before adding on a bit of preaching), they betray their misunderstanding of both worship and the act of preaching. Worship is not something we do before we settle down for the Word of God; it is the act through which the people of God direct all their attentiveness to hearing the one true and living God speak to His people and receive their praises. God is most beautifully praised when His people hear His Word, love His Word, and obey His Word.

As in the Reformation, the most important corrective to our corruption of worship (and defense against the consumerist demands of the day) is to return expository preaching and the public reading of God's Word to their rightful spot: to the heart of worship.

CHAPTER 5

A STEWARD OF MYSTERIES

The Preacher's Authority and Purpose

When the minister of the gospel faces the Lord God as judge, there will be many questions addressed to him, many standards of accountability, and many criteria of judgment. In the end, however, the most essential criterion of judgment for the minister of God will be, "Did you preach the Word? Did you fully carry out the ministry of the Word? In season and out of season, was the priority of your ministry the preaching of the Word?"

Of course this is not to say that there are not other issues, other responsibilities, and even other priorities. But it is to say that there is only one central, nonnegotiable, immovable, and essential priority, and that is the preaching of the Word of God.

The apostle Paul himself makes this clear in a majestic passage in Colossians 1:24–29. Here is what he writes:

> Now I rejoice in my sufferings for your sake, and in my flesh I am filling up what is lacking in Christ's afflictions for the sake of his body,

that is, the church, of which I became a minister according to the stewardship from God that was given to me for you, to make the word of God fully known, the mystery hidden for ages and generations but now revealed to his saints. To them God chose to make known how great among the Gentiles are the riches of the glory of this mystery, which is Christ in you, the hope of glory. Him we proclaim, warning everyone and teaching everyone with all wisdom, that we may present everyone mature in Christ. For this I toil, struggling with all his energy that he powerfully works within me.

Writing to the church in Colossae, Paul speaks here of his own understanding of the apostolic ministry, of his stewardship of the mysteries of God, and of his fulfilling of the task of proclaiming the Word of God. This is Paul's declaration of ministry, and he speaks of both the authority by which he preaches and the purpose of his preaching.

THE PREACHER'S AUTHORITY

Notice first that Paul sees himself as a servant of the Word of God. Look closely at the words of that paragraph. Paul is explaining why he so willingly submits to suffering—and indeed even rejoices in it! To anyone else, to speak of rejoicing in suffering would be ridiculous. But it makes perfect sense to Paul. He rejoices in suffering because his sufferings have earned him the opportunity to preach the gospel.

First and foremost, Paul sees himself as a servant of the Word of God, and he understands that his purpose on earth is to preach that Word and to proclaim Jesus Christ, even if it means he must suffer in order to do so.

In contrast to this gloriously counterintuitive outlook of Paul's, much of the contemporary church has simply given up on preaching. Rarely do we hear these days of a church that is distinguished primarily by its faithful, powerful, expository preaching. Instead, when we hear persons speak about their churches, they usually point to something other than preaching. They may speak of its specialized ministry to senior adults, or its children's ministry, or its youth ministry. They may speak of its music or its arts program or its drama team, or of things far more superficial than those. Sometimes they may even speak of the church's Great Commission vigor and its commitment to world missions—and for that we are certainly thankful. But, sadly, it is rare to hear a church described first and foremost by the character, power, and content of its preaching.

That is all the more striking because Paul is so clear in Colossians 1:25 about why he has been given his ministry. "Of [this church] I became a minister according to the stewardship from God that was given to me for you, to make the word of God fully known," he says. In the end, everything comes down to this. The central purpose of Paul's ministry, indeed the central purpose of every Christian ministry, is to make known the Word of God. The New American Standard translation of this verse actually says, "so that I might fully carry out *the preaching of* the Word of God." I believe that is a legitimate insertion. It is clear that what Paul means is that the "carrying out" of the Word of God is achieved by proclaiming, teaching, and preaching. Above everything else, that is the calling God had given him.

Along with that calling came a certain authority. If anything was clear in Paul's mind, it was that whatever authority and ministry he possessed did not originate in himself. He was called to it. It was given to him. "I became a minister," Paul says—or in other translations, "I *was made* a minister." Paul did not make himself a minister any more than he saved himself or appeared to himself on the Damascus Road. He was claimed by another, and he was made an apostle of the Lord Jesus and a minister of the Word. In fact, writing in 1 Corinthians 15:8, he explains that Christ appeared to him

> Far too many pastors assume that the authority they enjoy is their own, that they somehow earned it or achieved it.

"as to one untimely born." He was, in his own words, "the least of the apostles" because he had persecuted the church. Yet it was a sign of God's triumph in the gospel that He chose the chief persecutor of the church to become the Apostle to the Gentiles.

This fact is critical to the pastor's understanding of his calling and of the stewardship entrusted to him. Far too many pastors operate under the assumption that the authority they enjoy is their own, that they somehow earned it or achieved it, rather than merely receiving it from the hand of God. Similarly, the people in our churches are often fooled into trusting in the wrong kind of authority, an authority that originates in man and man's abilities rather than in the call of God.

There are three forms of false authority of which both pastors and churches should beware. First, there is *professional authority.* At the end of every semester at the seminary I lead, we award degrees and present diplomas to several hundred people. It is a solemn and important moment when that happens, but the reality is that those pieces of paper do not automatically confer on a person any special authority. Of course, the men and women who give themselves to learning are to be honored, but authority in the church is not finally a professional authority. The task of preaching and teaching the Word of God is not a profession to be represented by degrees and credentials and initials after one's name. It is a calling, given by the hand of God in grace, to men who do not and cannot deserve it.

Second, we must also beware of *positional authority*—that is, having authority merely because of our title or position in some structure or hierarchy. Martin Luther understood this point deeply. "Popes and councils may err," he insisted, "but my conscience is captive to the Word of God." No pastor should ever expect his congregation to follow him simply because he is The Pastor. Rather, he should lead them in the ways of God and expect them to follow him because he is following the Scriptures. Paul and Silas were not offended when the Bereans tested their message by the Scriptures (Acts 17:10–11). They did not insist that the Bereans ought to have accepted their message without question simply on the basis of their authority as apostles. Even the apostle Paul knew that his word was subject to the Word of God, and Luke called the Bereans "noble" for recognizing and acting on that fact.

Third, we must warn against *personal authority.* Some people have such charismatic personalities that they could lead persons to believe in virtually anything by sheer force of will. All around the world—whether in politics, ideology, or even spirituality and religion—there are charismatic leaders who have gathered around themselves tight cells of intensely loyal followers. Authority is in the teacher, and what the teacher says is taken as inviolable truth. Sadly, the church is not immune to this sort of false authority. There are many local churches whose pastors have installed themselves—or allowed themselves to be installed —as unquestionable authorities, not on the basis of the Word of God, but rather by the sheer force of personality and the ability to persuade or intimidate. That kind of personal authority was anathema to the apostle Paul. "If I, even I, should preach to you a different gospel, then anathematize me," he insists (Galatians 1:8, author's translation).

> We have been called out and granted a stewardship that we do not deserve and that we are not capable of fulfilling.

The preacher's authority lies not in profession, not in position, and not in personality. It lies in the Word of God alone.

THE PREACHER'S PURPOSE

Another critical point for the preacher to understand is that God has given him this calling not for his own benefit but for the benefit of the church. Look at what Paul says in Colossians 1:24: "I rejoice in my sufferings," he says, "for your sake." He ministered "for the sake of his body, that is, the church." Our calling to preach is a calling to serve others, and it is given to us entirely by God's grace. We have been called out and granted a stewardship that we do not deserve and that we are not capable of fulfilling. Nonetheless, God chooses us to carry it out. As Paul wrote:

> Where is the one who is wise? Where is the scribe? Where is the debater of this age? Has not God made foolish the wisdom of the world? But God chose what is foolish in the world to shame the wise; God chose what is weak in the world to shame the strong; God chose what is low and despised in the world, even things that are not, to bring to nothing things that are, so that no human being might boast in the presence of God.
>
> —1 CORINTHIANS 1:20, 27–29

Paul was under no illusions about the origin and authority of his ministry. He did not earn his ministry; it was given to him. His authority did not come from his position or personality; it flowed from the fact that he was proclaiming the Word of God.

What then was the aim of Paul's preaching? Why did he do it? Paul answers that question in Colossians 1:28: "Him we proclaim, warning everyone and teaching everyone with all wisdom, that we may present everyone mature in Christ." Paul's aim in his ministry of preaching the gospel was to present every Christian mature in Christ. What a job description! The aim of the pastor, of the one who preaches the Word of God, is that at the end of his ministry he might be able to present the Christians under his care complete and mature in their Savior.

To that end, we preach Christ in three ways. As Paul says in Colossians 1:28, we *proclaim* Christ, we *warn* people, and we *teach* people —all to the end of bringing Christians to maturity in Christ Jesus.

First, Paul says that his aim as a preacher is to *proclaim* Christ. That seems straightforward enough, but why does the apostle describe the content of his preaching as a "mystery"? The Word of God that he had been called to make fully known is, he says in verse 26, "the mystery hidden for ages and generations but now revealed to his saints." Throughout Asia Minor and the ancient world at this time, mystery religions and mystery cults were common. Many believed that Christianity was just another one of these mystery cults. After all, it too had its mystery, right? Yes, indeed. Go through the New Testament and see how many times the word "mystery" (*musterion*) appears. Obviously, Christianity does proclaim a mystery, but this is not a mystery of esoteric knowledge, or a Gnosticism consisting of some secret knowledge available only to elite intellectuals. No, Christianity's mystery is one that has been publicly revealed by God in the incarnation, death, burial, and resurrection of Jesus Christ.

Notice again what Paul says in verse 28. The "mystery" of the Christian gospel is really quite simple. "We proclaim *Him*," Paul says (NASB, italics added). We preach Christ; we proclaim Him; we focus our message on Him. That is a simple thing to say, but doing it requires painstaking, systematic, rigorous expository preaching. Our task is to show how Christ, the mystery of the ages, is revealed throughout the whole of Scripture, in both the Old Testament and the New. In other words, we have to paint the entire canvas with the truth of the mystery of Jesus Christ.

> The ultimate aim of preaching . . . the great glory of the Christian gospel is . . . "Christ in you, the hope of glory."

Too many preachers tend to work in one tiny corner of the great canvas of the work of God. The divine plan of redemption spans the ages, yet far too many preachers have made themselves specialists in this or that little corner of it. There are some preachers who, as painters, have only certain colors on their palette. Some have the vivid colors, others the more subdued colors. But in order to display for God's people the entire picture of God's plan for them, what is needed is the ability to paint the entire picture—in all its colors, all its hues, and all its shades. This means we ought to preach Christ from both the Old and the New Testaments, recognizing that, by the analogy of faith, every text in the entire Scripture points to Jesus Christ. It was the great Baptist preacher Charles Spurgeon who gave perhaps the best exhortation on this matter. "I take my text," he said, "and make a bee-line to the cross." In other words, even as we preach the immediate meaning of every text, we should also show its fulfillment in Jesus Christ.

When that happens, our congregations begin to see the whole astounding display of God's work of redemption. They understand its component parts and how they fit together. They understand the bright colors, and they see the subdued ones as well. Indeed, they understand the gospel in all its manifold glory. The mystery comes into focus.

Of course the ultimate aim of preaching is not merely to proclaim Christ as an abstract truth. The great glory of the Christian gospel is, as Paul says, "Christ in you, the hope of glory." This is explosive and transforming language. The gospel, according to the apostle Paul, is not simply offered to us on a platter for our consideration, our investigation, or our tasting. It is thrown at us with the power of hot, blazing rocks from a volcano. This is a living Word that we proclaim, one that is dangerous and life-changing. Paul's concern was not just that his hearers would come to a correct cognitive understanding of the gospel, although that was essential. His concern was that the gospel would be received by faith and that lives would be transformed as sinners become saints, enemies of God are justified by faith, and outcasts are adopted as sons and daughters of God. That is the power of preaching—of proclaiming Christ and Him crucified.

Second, Paul says that he intends with his preaching to *warn*. This issue of warning, or admonishing, is a rather difficult one in our day— a fact that is undeniable when we consider just how precious little admonishing actually goes on. Paul, however, described his ministry as one of admonishing.

What does it mean to admonish? Put starkly, it means to get in one's face. With our current ideas of personal privacy and personal autonomy, most of us today feel that no one has the right to tell us what to believe, how to act, or what we must correct in our behavior or thinking or actions. After all, we say, "My marriage is *my* marriage. My job is a matter between me and my employer, and no one else has the right to stick his nose into it." That is hardly the pattern in the New Testament, however. When the Word of God is authentically preached, it is also applied. I do not mean that the preacher searches for some way to make the text relevant. I mean rather that the text must be directly addressed to persons in the congregation: "This is what you must do. This is what you must think. This is who you must be."

Isaac Backus, the great eighteenth-century Baptist, started his ministry as an exhorter. In revolutionary America, the exhorter had a particular task in the congregation. After the preacher had preached, it was his responsibility to apply the message. This might mean going up to someone and saying, "Now, Widow Jones, this means you are going to have to change the way you raise your children." Or, "Mister Smith, you are going to have to change the way you do business."

Backus was fifteen years old when he took on the assignment of being an exhorter, which, given the responsibilities of the job, is probably an indication of the church's recognition that fifteen-year-olds are uniquely willing to do dangerous things—and perhaps that they considered Backus to be particularly expendable too! The point is that this congregation took seriously the call to admonition. They understood that they were called, together, to be accountable to the Word of God in everything that they did and thought.

> It's crucial we reclaim the truth that one role of the preacher is to expose error and to reveal sin.

I am not calling for a similar system in churches today. I only speak of Backus to point out that there is not much admonishment happening in local churches today. In fact, this kind of warning and admonishment would most likely be seen as intolerant, invasive, and even arrogant. Even so, it is crucial we reclaim the truth that one role of the preacher is to expose error and to reveal sin. In 2 Timothy 3:16–17, Paul tells Timothy that as he preaches the Word he is to rebuke and to correct. He is to take it upon himself to tell people that they are wrong, and that their thinking needs to be brought into alignment with Scripture.

Sadly, the failure of this task of correcting, rebuking, and admonishing has led to many churches having become little more than voluntary associations with a steeple. That ought not to be the case. If we are to remain faithful to the task of preaching the Word of God and of presenting every Christian mature in Christ, it will require that we find again the courage to warn and admonish.

Third, Paul says that the task of preaching involves *teaching*, or more specifically, instructing the people of God about the Scriptures and applying those Scriptures to their lives. Teaching is not something that can be sequestered in the Sunday school. We cannot assume that the teaching ministry of the church is fulfilled when you have a good children's education system. The teaching of the Word of God should be cross-generational. Moreover, it should be progressive and accumulative, so that the saints are brought into greater maturity in the Lord Jesus Christ. Furthermore, the teaching of the Word of God is to comfort.

The awesome power of authentic preaching is seen in the fact that God uses preaching to present His saints complete in Christ. How are Christians going to grow? How are they going to be matured? How is the process of Holy Spirit–directed sanctification going to be seen in them? All by the preaching of the Word.

When we finally come to heaven, in the presence of the Lord Jesus, that is when the product of our labors will finally be visible. Then we will see the saints to whom we preached clothed in the righteousness of Christ—men and women, brothers and sisters in Christ, made complete in Him and glorifying Him for all eternity. That is our task, and that is our aim. When we ask the question whether or not we are successful in ministry, we must answer that question by this criterion alone. Are we seeing the saints grow to completeness in Jesus Christ?

CHAPTER 6

"DID NOT OUR HEARTS BURN WITHIN US?"

Preaching the Bible's Big Story

I remember as a child singing the song about Zaccheus and his sycamore tree. "Zaccheus was a wee little man, and a wee little man was he." One of the great problems with much evangelical preaching today, and one of the reasons so many saints are not growing to completeness in Jesus Christ, is that so many of our pulpits are filled with what you might call "Zaccheus sermons"—or to put it more bluntly, wee little preaching.

Every Sunday, far too many preachers read a wee little text, apply it in wee little ways to their people's lives, and then tell everyone to come back next week for another wee little story.

That tendency to isolate our sermons to one tiny piece of biblical text is a major problem, and it also explains why so much evangelical preaching is moralistic. It is easy to pick out a familiar story, make a few points from it about what people should and should not do, and then be done with it. But that kind of preaching will leave a church weak and starving, because the Christians who sit under it never find themselves in the big story of God's work in the world. If we as preachers want to see our people growing to maturity in Christ, we must give them more than a diet of wee little morality sermons. We must place every text we preach firmly within the grand, sweeping story of the Bible.

REJECTING THE BIG STORY

One of the challenges of preaching in the postmodern age is that most of the people around us have rejected the idea of the big story altogether. They deny that there can be any one overarching "meta-narrative" to which all other narratives are accountable. Jean Francois Lyotard, the chief French theorist of postmodernity, defined post-modernism this way: "Simplifying to the extreme, I define postmod-ernism as incredulity toward metanarratives."[1] What he meant was that people no longer believe that there is one big story to which all our own individual stories are accountable. All that exists, in other words, are the little stories of each individual person or culture.

The effect of this rejection of metanarratives has been especially pronounced in the academy. In France, for instance, academic histo-rians have stopped looking at the big story of history—the grand movements and the great leaders—and have begun studying instead what they called *petite histoire*, or "little histories." Thus if you read re-cent French historical works, you are more likely to read about the personal experiences of a thirteenth-century milkmaid than about the history of medieval civilization. Academic historians have lost confi-dence that there is a big story to tell, and therefore they have just set-tled for telling the little stories.

The prevailing "incredulity toward metanarratives" is a big story itself, ironically, and it helps to explain a good deal. It explains, for in-stance, why there was intellectual and spiritual exhaustion at the end of the twentieth century, for the twentieth century was a battle of competing metanarratives. One of the century's great conflicts in fact was that between democratic liberalism and Communism—the idea of a representative democracy in which people are accorded basic liberties and civil rights, over against the idea that the basic dynamic of human existence is economic oppression from which people must be liberated by the power of revolution.

COMMUNISM AND OTHER FAILED METANARRATIVES

Communism, or Marxism, was one of the twentieth century's metanarratives. It explained everything: Where did it all begin? What went wrong? Can it be fixed? Where is it all heading? Communism had answers to all these questions. Based on a naturalistic worldview, Communism declared that there was no greater meaning to life or existence and thus no overarching reality to challenge Communism's own primacy. To the question, "What went wrong," Communism answered "Economic oppression." This is the fall, according to Marxist theory, and it amounts not to sin, but to economic inequality and oppression. Can it be fixed? Yes, answered the Marxists, the problem can be fixed by revolution—by an uprising in which the proletariat would seize the means of production and liberate themselves from their oppressors.

There is an eschatology to Marxism as well, a belief that history was heading to a permanent, stable state of revolution with power in the hands of a few. Communism failed intellectually at least in part because its eschatology became untenable. The promised state of liberation never came, and starving people grew tired of waiting for it.

There were other metanarratives in the twentieth century that failed, too. Fascism was one. The faith in human progress that marked the early decades of the century was another. Indeed by the end of the twentieth century, there was exhaustion even with defending the Western metanarrative of freedom and democracy. And in the wake of all this, many people simply gave up on the idea of one overarching, all-encompassing story altogether and declared that any claim to such a metanarrative was simply delusion.

A GRAND STORY THAT EXPLAINS
ALL OTHER STORIES

That is why Christianity comes as such a threat to so many people, for the Christian story is a metanarrative—a grand story that explains all other stories, and to which all other stories must answer. As Christians, we actually claim that we are possessed by the one story to which all other stories are accountable. Thus when we share the Christian gospel with someone, we say, "Yes, I want to hear your story. But more important, I want your story to be absorbed within a different, larger story. I want to place your story—your *petite histoire*—into the sweeping metanarrative of what God is doing in the world, so that you might know Jesus Christ as Savior and Lord, and thus know where you are and who you are in a whole different way."

When we preach, we must remember that what we proclaim is not just a little story, and not just a series of little stories. It is the big picture. We are accountable to the big story of God's work as it is narrated in Scripture.

In Luke 24, the resurrected Jesus introduces two of His disciples to Scripture's grand narrative. In other words, he imposes a metanarrative:

> That very day two of them were going to a village named Emmaus, about seven miles from Jerusalem, and they were talking with each other about all these things that had happened. While they were talking and discussing together, Jesus himself drew near and went with them. But their eyes were kept from recognizing him. And he said to them, "What is this conversation that you are holding with each other as you walk?" And they stood still, looking sad. Then one of them, named Cleopas, answered him, "Are you the only visitor to Jerusalem who does not know the things that have happened there in these days?" And he said to them, "What things?" And they said to him, "Concerning Jesus of Nazareth, a man who was a prophet mighty in deed and word before God and all the people, and how our chief priests and rulers delivered him up to be condemned to

death, and crucified him. But we had hoped that he was the one to redeem Israel. Yes, and besides all this, it is now the third day since these things happened. Moreover, some women of our company amazed us. They were at the tomb early in the morning, and when they did not find his body, they came back saying that they had even seen a vision of angels, who said that he was alive. Some of those who were with us went to the tomb and found it just as the women had said, but him they did not see." And he said to them, "O foolish ones, and slow of heart to believe all that the prophets have spoken! Was it not necessary that the Christ should suffer these things and enter into his glory?" And beginning with Moses and all the Prophets, he interpreted to them in all the Scriptures the things concerning himself.

So they drew near to the village to which they were going. He acted as if he were going farther, but they urged him strongly, saying, "Stay with us, for it is toward evening and the day is now far spent." So he went in to stay with them. When he was at table with them, he took the bread and blessed and broke it and gave it to them. And their eyes were opened, and they recognized him. And he vanished from their sight. They said to each other, "Did not our hearts burn within us while he talked to us on the road, while he opened to us the Scriptures?" (verses 13–32)

In this passage, we are told of two disciples of Jesus who were walking from Jerusalem to a village called Emmaus. It was a significant walk—about seven miles—so there would have been ample time for conversation. As they were walking, the two disciples were discussing the events that had just taken place in Jerusalem. Just at that moment, Jesus Himself approached and began traveling with them, though "their eyes were kept from recognizing him" (verse 16). Jesus asked them, "What is this conversation that you are holding with each other as you walk?"

The question clearly struck them, for they stopped walking and looked very sad. What an amazing moment! Here was Jesus—the resurrected and victorious Lord—standing right beside these two disciples, and yet they were filled with sadness and looked at the ground. The irony here is thick, isn't it? These disciples wouldn't have been sad if they had know who it was standing beside them!

After a moment, one of the disciples, Cleopas, answered him: "Are you the only person in Jerusalem who hasn't heard of this? Where have you been? These things are headline news!" And then they described specifically "the things about Jesus the Nazarene, who was a prophet, mighty in deed and word in the sight of God and in the sight of all the people, and how our chief priests and rulers delivered him up and crucified him." Here we learn the reason for their sadness: "We had hoped that he was the one to redeem Israel."

Even so, there were rumors floating around that very day. Some of the believing women had been to Jesus' tomb early that morning, and had come back saying it was empty and that they had also seen a vision of an angel saying that Jesus was risen. Moreover, they told this stranger, "Some of those who were with us went to the tomb and found things just as the women said, but they didn't see Jesus."

Our people can have a deep repository of biblical facts and stories, and yet know nothing about how any of it fits together.

As far as these disciples knew, that was the end of the story. All the dramatic happenings in Jerusalem of the past few days had come to an end—which is probably why they were leaving for Emmaus—and the most they could say was that it had all ended with a question mark: some rumors, some circumstantial evidence, some hints and shadows, but no Jesus.

But then Jesus speaks to them a word of rebuke, one based on the fact that as Jews, as the covenant people of God, they had Moses and the prophets, and therefore they should have understood more than they did. "O foolish ones," Jesus says, "and slow of heart to believe all that the prophets have spoken!"

"Why are you confused about this?" Jesus seems to say. "Didn't you read the Bible?" And then starting with Moses—that is, at the very beginning of the Old Testament—and moving through all the prophets, Jesus preached to these disciples about Himself. He taught them everything the Old Testament had to say about him.

Hours later, when Jesus broke the bread and they finally recognized him, the two disciples realized what had just happened to them—the risen Christ Himself had been teaching them from the Old Testament. So they said to each other, "Did not our hearts burn within us while he talked to us on the road, while he opened to us the Scriptures?"

Now that is an incredible question! Here is the miracle, the mystery, and the majesty of preaching. People who have heard the Word of God preached should leave asking questions like this, or like the one God spoke through Moses in Deuteronomy 4: "Did any people ever hear the voice of God speaking out of the midst of the fire, as you have heard, and still live?" (verse 33)

That is what each of us should desire to see happening, and yet this is one of the great weaknesses of so much evangelical preaching in these days. Our people can know so much, and yet know nothing, all at the same time. They can have a deep repository of biblical facts and stories, and yet know absolutely nothing about how any of it fits together, or why any of it matters beyond the wee little "moral of the story."

THE SWEEPING STORY OF JESUS

Even more, the moralistic fables that many evangelicals hear from their pastors week in and week out will not evoke the kind of burning-in-the-heart awe that these two disciples experienced on the road to Emmaus. If we want our people to feel that kind of excitement about the gospel, then they need to hear and know the same sweeping story that Jesus unfolded to these two disciples.

"Beginning with Moses and all the Prophets," Luke says, "he interpreted to them in all the Scriptures the things concerning himself." Every single text of Scripture points to Jesus Christ. He is the Lord of all, and therefore He is the Lord of the Scriptures too. From Moses to the prophets, He is the focus of every single word of the Bible. Every verse of Scripture finds its fulfillment in Him, and every story in the Bible ends with Him. That is what our people need to understand—that the Bible is not just a compendium of good short stories, but a grand, life-encompassing metanarrative of God's work of redemption in the world.

Every time we preach a text of Scripture, we are accountable to that text. We must read and explain accurately to our people what that text means and how it applies to their lives. Yet we have another task as well, for we must take that particular text and place it within the larger story of Scripture. One of the reasons I encourage pastors to preach through entire books of the Bible is because that practice will force us to preach texts we otherwise would never preach. If we reduce our preaching ministry to "Highlights from the Book of Romans," we can be sure there will be parts of Romans that won't be highlighted. Similarly, if you only look at the highlights of the Pentateuch, you'll preach the famous stories, but you'll probably also miss what the Holy Spirit has to say through much of Leviticus. Chapter after chapter of regulations about sacrifices, offerings, washings, purifications, and the like does not seem at first to make for good, exciting sermons. Yet all that concern for purity in sacrifice is a crucial part of the Christian story. It was pointing to the ultimate sacrifice of the perfectly obedient One, who shed His blood so that we could be forgiven once for all. Jesus paid it all. His blood washes clean.

That is why the book of Leviticus is important, and why we need to preach it even if it's not filled with dramatic stories. Do our people

> Every text—not just the ones we know well—cries out about the Lord Jesus Christ.

feel the burden and weight of sin that called for such detailed regulations and rituals? Do they feel the release and exaltation of not having to do these things every day, of not having to sit outside the tent, of not having to worry about being ritually unclean? By the power of the gospel, there is no one who needs to be unclean or unrighteous in God's sight, for sinners are washed once for all in the blood of the Lamb. Every text—not just the ones we know well—cries out about the Lord Jesus Christ.

Let me offer a framework for thinking about how individual biblical texts fit into Scripture's big story. The Bible's storyline consists of at least four great movements that are absolutely necessary: *creation, fall, redemption,* and *consummation.* Without these four movements, we cannot understand ourselves as human beings or our place in God's work. With them, we can understand the entire sweep of Scripture's story.

THE STORY'S FIRST MOVEMENT: CREATION

Every worldview, every metanarrative, has a beginning. If we are to say anything meaningful about the world and where it is going, we must first know how it all started.

Today, two stark alternatives seek to explain how all this came to be, and the implications of these two worldviews are all-encompassing. First, there is the naturalistic account of the world's origin, the materialistic evolutionary assertion that everything that exists is simply and merely an accident. On the other hand is the biblical testimony, which declares that "In the beginning, God created the heavens and the earth." The divergence between those two assertions is enormous, so huge in fact that it is beyond our comprehension. For if we believe that God the Creator—the omnipotent and omniscient One—created the world and human beings as the theater of His glory, then we will approach all of life in a manner completely different than if we believe that all this is merely an accident, that matter and time and energy produced all of this by chance.

The most important divergence between the biblical worldview and a naturalistic worldview is the place of human beings. Are we merely some kind of biological accident in the midst of a cosmological accident? Or are we, as Scripture teaches, the only creatures made in the image of God, and therefore the only ones with the ability to know God and have a sense of accountability to Him? How you answer that question will affect everything else you do in life—from sexuality to the sanctity of life to the purposefulness of our labor to the meaning of life itself. This is, quite literally, the most basic and most fundamental of questions: Are we made for a purpose, or are we the accidental product of a chaotic universe?

Of course the answer is that God did indeed create all we see, and we ourselves are created in God's image. As the image-bearers of God, we thus understand that there is an inherent purpose in our existence, a grander and more glorious purpose than any we could imagine. Understanding that beginning, and constantly reminding our people of it, is a crucial part of our task as preachers. One way or another, our people need to be reminded in every sermon that this story has a beginning, and that this beginning has everything to do with the glory of God. This world has dignity and meaning because God created it. We have dignity and meaning because God created us. What is more, we have a special status and purpose in God's plan because He created us in His image, and determined that this one creature—human beings—would consciously know and worship him.

THE STORY'S SECOND MOVEMENT: FALL

Of course the fact that God created the world does not explain everything we experience. So soon after the creation in Genesis 1 comes the story of the fall in Genesis 3. We cannot understand anything about ourselves in our present condition without immediate reference to this. Indeed, it is the fall into sin that explains all the suffering, all the strife, all the pain and conflict in our lives. Yet many evangelical preachers make so little reference to it that our people are left without the tools they need to understand their lives—and more importantly, their deep need for salvation.

Without a robust understanding of the fall and its effects, our people cannot understand their lives or the world around them. They cannot understand the fallenness of human society, nor that the creation itself is groaning under the effects of sin.

Why is it that so many Christians can have their faith rocked in the wake of a natural disaster? Why are they left asking the question "Where was God?" as if God somehow messed up by allowing this to happen? Why are so many Christians driven to shocked despair when elected officials don't bring the results they expected, or when the culture continues its march into depravity despite their best efforts? The reason is because those Christians do not understand the fall.

Sure, they know about Adam and Eve and the forbidden fruit. They have heard of the serpent and how he seduced Eve into taking a bite, and they know that Eve then gave it to Adam. They may even know a bit about what God said in the aftermath, but what they do not understand is the importance, the catastrophic significance, of that sin.

The fall was not just an individual peccadillo. It changed everything. When sin entered into the experience of the cosmos, everything was affected by it. Thus when God pronounces His verdict against Adam, He tells him that even the earth now will become hostile. It will fight against Adam for its harvest. Adam would have to work—hard—for the earth would not yield its produce to him willingly. Moreover, in the pain of childbirth, Eve would be reminded of the fall and her sin. Even in the glorious generation of life there would be the sharp reminder of humanity's fallenness. Finally, because of their sin Adam and Eve would be expelled from paradise. What God had made for them, and for us, was lost. We are blocked from seeing it, prevented from experiencing it, prohibited from eating from the Tree of Life.

Where once human beings walked with God in the cool of the day and joyfully cultivated a garden created for their enjoyment, now we are aliens in a hostile land. Rather than being creatures who worship God in the perfection of Eden, naked and unashamed before Him, we are now reduced to weaving fig leaves together to try to cover our own nakedness. We are ashamed, because we cannot even look at ourselves without understanding that we are marred by a deep and profound corruption.

Really, that is the only way we can understand ourselves, the only way we can deal with what we see in the mirror. If we think we are essentially good—or even morally neutral—beings, we delude ourselves. The fall explains why we are who we are, why we do what we do, why we hide what we hide. It explains why human society is as it is, why entertainment is as it is, why our spouses are as they are. It explains why our children do not need to be taught how to sin, and why we have locks on our doors. It explains why we are never satisfied, never content, never truly at peace.

Most importantly, the fall explains why we are spiritually dead, and why we deserve to be. For condemnation and eternal judgment is the only just response of a holy God to the reality of who we are and what we have done.

THE STORY'S THIRD MOVEMENT: REDEMPTION

If we were left with the fall as the end of the story, nihilism would be the only appropriate response. Eat, drink, and be merry, for tomorrow we die. But there is a third movement in the Bible's storyline: redemption. What we could not do for ourselves, God did. In order to bring even greater glory to himself, God acted to save us from our own sin.

Looking back over the Bible's story, we now recognize that it is a much bigger story than we could have imagined at the beginning. By redeeming sinners, God glorifies Himself and declares His holiness in a way we would never have known if we simply knew Him as Creator. God is not *just* our Creator; He is our Creator *and* our Redeemer!

When Paul writes in 1 Corinthians 5:21 that "For our sake he made him to be sin who knew no sin, so that in him we might become the righteousness of God," he is talking about a cosmological reversal that is beyond anything we can understand. If our people think of the gospel as a small story in which they get to befriend Jesus and walk alone with Him in a garden, if they don't understand what a massive thing their salvation from sin really is, then we are robbing them of the gospel.

Every time we preach, we need to create dissonance in the minds of our hearers. We need to declare our wretchedness, our sin, and our powerlessness, and we need to admit frankly that we can't solve this problem. And then we proclaim the gospel. We show our people how God Himself did what they were wholly unable to do. We tell them that the problem of sin was only solved when the sinless Son of God died on the cross as a substitute for His people.

THE STORY'S FINAL MOVEMENT: CONSUMMATION

Redemption is as cosmic as sin and its effect. Indeed we fail to really preach the gospel in its awesome massiveness unless we point to the fact that God is about not only redeeming sinners but also creating a new heaven and a new earth. He is not merely restoring the world to the paradise of Eden, but creating something that will be greater than the garden ever was. Consummation is not just a return to where we began. It is God preparing for us what no eye has seen, nor ear heard, nor the heart of man ever imagined (1 Corinthians 2:9).

The vision of consummation held out at the end of the book of Revelation is greater than Genesis ever knew. The new heaven and the new earth will be even greater than that which God Himself declared to be "very good." How could that be? How could the new creation be better than the original, very good one? It will be better because God's glory will be more magnificently demonstrated.

Look at the progression in Revelation 4 and 5. The apostle John writes in chapter 4 that the living creatures never cease to say, "Holy,

holy, holy is the Lord God Almighty, who was and is and is to come!"
The twenty-four elders cast their crowns before him and sing, "Worthy are you, our Lord and God, to receive glory and honor and power, for you created all things, and by your will they existed and were created!" (verses 8, 10–11). They are praising God as Creator.

But something more is added in chapter 5. When the Lion of the tribe of Judah, the Root of David, is revealed as a slain Lamb with the power to open the scroll, the living creatures and the twenty-four elders sing a new song: "Worthy are you to take the scroll and to open its seals, for you were slain, and by your blood you ransomed people for God from every tribe and language and people and nation, and you have made them a kingdom and priests to our God, and they shall reign on the earth" (verses 9–10). Here they praise God not only as Creator, but also as Redeemer.

In the garden of Eden, Adam and Eve certainly knew many songs they could sing of God's glory of Creator, but they did not know to sing "Worthy is the Lamb!" We are more privileged than Adam and Even were in the garden. We get to sing "Worthy is the Lamb who was slain!"

TELLING THE WHOLE STORY

Many of our people are dying of spiritual starvation because they do not know the Bible's whole story, and thus they do not find themselves in the story. True, they know many little stories. They have a bag of facts. But a little bit of knowledge is not a big picture. As we preach, we need to bring every text into accountability with the big story of Scripture. When you preach, help your people to know the beginning, the middle, and the end—creation, fall, redemption, and consummation. In doing so, you will show your people who they are and where they are going. You will help them to incorporate their little stories into God's grand metanarrative, and you will help them press on with burning hearts toward maturity and completeness in Christ.

We want our people to leave the preaching event asking the right questions. If our preaching is too small, their questions will be equally small. If we neglect the big story—the gospel metanarrative—they will be satisfied with small questions and will live on small insights. They may take home an insight, a story, a principle, or perhaps an anecdote. We should not be satisfied with that. They should not be satisfied with that. Our ambition—our obsession as preachers—should be nothing less than to preach so that the congregation sees the big story of the gospel, the grand narrative of the gospel, through every text we preach.

In other words, let us pray that they just might ask, given the power of the Word of God: "Did our hearts not burn within us, as the Scriptures were explained to us?"

CHAPTER 7

THE PASTOR AS THEOLOGIAN
Preaching and Doctrine

Every pastor is called to be a theologian. This may come as a surprise to those pastors who see theology as an academic discipline taken during seminary rather than as an ongoing and central part of the pastoral calling. Nevertheless, the health of the church depends upon its pastors functioning as faithful theologians—teaching, preaching, defending, and applying the great doctrines of the faith.

One of the most lamentable developments of the last several centuries has been theology's transformation into an academic discipline more associated with the university than the church. In the earliest eras of the church, and indeed throughout the annals of Christian history, the central theologians of the church were its pastors. Athanasius, Irenaeus, and Augustine were all pastors of churches, even as they are revered as some of early Christianity's greatest theologians. Similarly, the great theologians of the Reformation were, in the main, pastors such as John Calvin and Martin Luther. Of course, their responsibilities often ranged beyond those of the average pastor, but they could not have conceived of the pastoral role without the essential stewardship of theology.

The emergence of theology as an academic discipline coincides with the development of the modern university. Of course, theology was one of the three major disciplines taught in the medieval university. Yet, so long as the medieval synthesis between nature and grace was commonly understood, the university was always seen to be in direct service to the church and its pastors.

The rise of the modern research university led to the development of theology as merely one academic discipline among others—and eventually to the redefinition of theology as "religious studies" separated from ecclesiastical control or concern. In most universities, the secularization of the academy has meant that the academic discipline of theology has no inherent connection to Christianity, much less to its central truth claims.

These developments have caused great harm to the church, separating ministry from theology, preaching from doctrine, and Christian care from conviction. In far too many cases, the pastor's ministry has been evacuated of serious doctrinal content, and many pastors seem to have little connection to any sense of theological vocation. All this must be reversed if the church is to remain true to God's Word and the gospel. Unless the pastor functions as a theologian, theology is left in the hands of those who, in many cases, have little or no connection or commitment to the local church.

THE PASTOR'S CALLING

The pastoral calling is inherently theological. Given the fact that the pastor is to be the teacher of the Word of God and the teacher of the gospel, it cannot be otherwise. The idea of the pastorate as a non-theological office is inconceivable in light of the New Testament.

Though this truth is implicit throughout the Scriptures, it is perhaps most apparent in Paul's letters to Timothy. In these short and powerful letters, Paul establishes Timothy's role as a theologian and also affirms that all of Timothy's fellow pastors are to share in the same calling. Paul emphatically encourages Timothy concerning his reading, teaching, preaching, and study of Scripture. All of this is essentially theological, as is made clear when Paul commands Timothy to "follow the pattern of the sound words that you have heard from me, in the faith and love that are in Christ Jesus. By the Holy Spirit who dwells within us, guard the good deposit entrusted to you" (2 Timothy 1:13–14). Timothy is to be a teacher of others who will also teach. "What you have heard from me in the presence of many witnesses entrust to faithful men who will be able to teach others also" (2 Timothy 2:2).

As Paul completes his second letter to Timothy, he reaches a crescendo of concern as he commands him to preach the Word, specifically instructing him to "reprove, rebuke, and exhort, with complete patience and teaching" (4:2). Why? "For the time is coming when people will not endure sound teaching, but having itching ears they will accumulate for themselves teachers to suit their own passions, and will turn away from listening to the truth and wander off into myths" (4:3–4).

> The pastor's calling is . . . deeply, inherently, and inescapably theological.

Further, Paul defines the duty of the overseer or pastor as one who is "holding fast the faithful word which is in accordance with the teaching, so that he will be able both to exhort in sound doctrine and to refute those who contradict" (Titus 1:9 NASB). In this single verse, Paul simultaneously affirms the apologetic and polemical facets of the pastor-theologian's calling. As he makes clear, the pastoral theologian must be able to defend the faith even as he identifies false teachings and makes correction by the Word of God. There is no more theological calling than this—guard the flock of God for the sake of God's truth.

In fact, there is no dimension of the pastor's calling that is *not* deeply, inherently, and inescapably theological. There is no problem the pastor will encounter in counseling that is not specifically theological in character. There is no major question in ministry that does not come with deep theological dimensions and the need for careful theological application. The task of leading, feeding, and guiding the congregation is as theological as any other conceivable vocation.

Evangelism is a theological calling as well, for the very act of sharing the gospel is, in short, a theological argument presented with the goal of seeing a sinner come to faith in the Lord Jesus Christ. In order to be a faithful evangelist, the pastor must first understand the gospel and then understand the nature of the evangelist's calling. At every step of the way, the pastor is dealing with issues that are irrefutably theological.

Most important, the preaching and teaching of the Word of God is theological from beginning to end. The preacher functions as a steward of the mysteries of God, explaining the deepest and most profound theological truths to a congregation that must be armed with the knowledge of these truths in order to grow as disciples and meet the challenge of faithfulness in the Christian life.

As many observers have noted, today's pastors are often pulled in many directions simultaneously—and the theological vocation is often lost amidst the pressing concerns of a ministry that has been reconceived as something other than what Paul intended for Timothy. The managerial revolution has left many pastors feeling more like administrators than theologians, dealing with matters of organizational theory before ever turning to the deep truths of God's Word and the application of these truths to everyday life. The rise of therapeutic concerns within the culture means that many pastors, and many of their church members, believe that the pastoral calling is best understood as a "helping profession." As such, the pastor is seen as someone who functions in a therapeutic role in which theology is often seen as more of a problem than a solution.

All this is a betrayal of the pastoral calling as presented in the New

Testament. Furthermore, it is a rejection of the apostolic teaching and of the biblical admonition concerning the role and responsibilities of the pastor. Today's pastors must recover and reclaim the pastoral calling as inherently and cheerfully *theological*. Otherwise, pastors will be nothing more than communicators, counselors, and managers of congregations that have been emptied of the gospel and of biblical truth.

THE PASTOR'S CONCENTRATION

Being faithful to this theological task will obviously require intense and self-conscious theological thinking, study, and concentration. If the church is to be marked by faithful preaching, God-honoring worship, and effective evangelism, the pastor must give concentrated attention to the theological task. Part of that thinking is the ability to isolate what is most important in terms of theological gravity from that which is less important.

This is what I call the process of *theological triage.* As anyone who visits a hospital emergency room is aware, a triage nurse is customarily in place to make a first-stage evaluation of which patients are most in need of care. A patient with a gunshot wound is cared for ahead of a sprained ankle. This makes perfect medical sense, and indeed to ignore this sense of priority would amount to medical malpractice! In a similar manner, the pastor must learn to discern different levels of theological importance. I identify three distinct orders of doctrine in terms of importance.

First-order doctrines are those that are fundamental and essential to the Christian faith. The pastor's theological instincts should seize upon any compromise of doctrines such as the full deity and humanity of Christ, the doctrine of the Trinity, the doctrine of atonement, and essentials such as justification by faith alone. Where such doctrines are compromised, the Christian faith falls. When a pastor hears an assertion that it is not necessary to believe in Christ's bodily resurrection from the dead, he must respond with a theological instinct that recognizes such a denial as tantamount to a rejection of the gospel itself.

Second-order doctrines are those that are essential to church life and necessary for the ordering of the local church, but that, in themselves, do not define the gospel. That is to say, one may detect an error in a doctrine at this level and still acknowledge that the person in error remains a believing Christian. Nevertheless, such doctrines are directly related to how the church is organized and its ministry is fulfilled. Doctrines at this level include those most closely related to ecclesiology and the architecture of theological systems. Evangelical baptists and paedobaptists, for example, disagree concerning a number of vital and urgently important doctrines—most crucially whether the Bible teaches that the infants of believers should be baptized. Yet both can acknowledge each other as genuine Christians, even though these differences have such immediate practical implications that it would be impossible to function together in a single local congregation.

Congregations that are fed nothing more than ambiguous "principles" supposedly drawn from God's Word are doomed to a spiritual immaturity.

Third-order doctrines are those that may be the ground for fruitful theological discussion and debate, but that do not threaten the fellowship of the local congregation or denomination. For example, Christians who agree on an entire range of theological issues and doctrines may disagree over matters related to the timing and sequence of events related to Christ's return. Yet such debates, while still deeply important because of their biblical nature and connection to the gospel, do not constitute a ground for separation among believing Christians.

Without a proper sense of priority and discernment, the congregation is left to consider every theological issue to be a matter of potential conflict or, at the other extreme, to see no doctrines as worth defending if conflict is in any way possible. The pastor's theological concentration establishes a sense of proper proportion and a larger frame of theological reference. At the same time, this concentration on the theological dimension of ministry also reminds the pastor of the necessity of constant watchfulness.

At crucial points in the history of Christian theology, the difference between orthodoxy and heresy has often hung on a single word, or even a syllable. When Arius argued that the Son was to be understood as being of a *similar* substance as the Father, Athanasius correctly understood that the entirety of the gospel was at risk. As Athanasius faithfully led the church to understand, the New Testament clearly teaches that the Son is of the same substance as the Father. In the Greek language, the distinction between the word offered by Arius and the correction offered by Athanasius was a single syllable. Looking back, we can now see that when the Council of Nicaea met in AD 325, the gospel was defended and defined at this very point. Without the role of Athanasius as both pastor and theologian, the heresy of Arius might have spread unchecked, leading to disaster for the young church.

THE PASTOR'S CONVICTION

As a theologian, the pastor must be known for what he teaches as well as for what he knows, affirms, and believes. The health of the church depends upon pastors who infuse their congregations with deep biblical and theological conviction, and the primary means of this transfer of conviction is the preaching of the Word of God.

We will be hard-pressed to define any activity as being more inherently theological than the preaching of God's Word, for preaching is an exercise in the theological exposition of Scripture. Congregations that are fed nothing more than ambiguous "principles" supposedly drawn from God's Word are doomed to a spiritual immaturity that will quickly become visible in compromise, complacency, and a host of other spiritual ills.

Why else would the apostle Paul command Timothy to preach the Word in such solemn and serious terms? "I charge you in the presence of God and of Christ Jesus, who is to judge the living and the dead, and by his appearing and his kingdom: preach the word; be ready in season and out of season; reprove, rebuke, and exhort, with complete patience and teaching" (2 Timothy 4:1–2).

As we have already seen, this very text points to the inescapably theological character of ministry. In these preceding verses, Paul specifically ties this theological ministry to the task of preaching—understood to be the pastor's supreme calling. As Martin Luther rightly affirmed, the preaching of the Word of God is the first mark of the church. Where it is found, there one finds the church. Where it is absent, there is no church, whatever others may claim.

If Scripture is truly "breathed out [i.e., inspired] by God and profitable for teaching, for reproof, for correction, and for training in righteousness" (2 Timothy 3:16), then it is through the expository preaching of the Word of God that biblical knowledge is imparted to the congregation, and God's people are armed with deep theological conviction. In other words, the pastor's conviction about theological preaching becomes the foundation for the transfer of these convictions into the hearts of God's people. The divine agent of this transfer is the Holy Spirit, who opens hearts, eyes, and ears to hear, understand, and receive the Word of God. But the preacher has a responsibility too—to be clear, specific, systematic, and comprehensive in setting out the biblical truth that will frame a biblical understanding of the Christian faith and the Christian life.

THE PASTOR'S CONFESSION

All this assumes, of course, that the pastoral ministry is first rooted in the pastor's own confession of faith—the pastor's personal theological convictions. The faithful pastor does not teach merely that which has historically been believed by the church and is now believed by faithful Christians. Rather, he teaches out of his own personal confession of belief. There can be no theological detachment or sense of academic distance when the pastor sets out a theological vision of the Christian life.

All true Christian preaching is experiential preaching, set before the congregation by a man who is possessed by deep theological passion, specific theological convictions, and an eagerness to see these convictions shared by his congregation. That is why faithful preaching cannot consist in the preacher simply presenting a set of theological options to the congregation. Instead, the pastor should stand ready to define, defend, and document his own deep convictions, drawn from his careful study of God's Word and his knowledge of the faithful teaching of the church.

> The pastor should stand ready to define, defend, and document his own deep convictions.

Once again, our model for this kind of pastoral confidence is the apostle Paul. Throughout the New Testament, Paul's personal testimony is intertwined with his own theology. Consider Paul's retrospective analysis of his own attempts at human righteousness, coupled with his bold embrace of the gospel as grounded in grace alone. "But whatever gain I had, I counted as loss for the sake of Christ," Paul asserted.

> Indeed, I count everything as loss because of the surpassing worth of knowing Christ Jesus my Lord. For his sake I have suffered the loss of all things and count them as rubbish, in order that I may gain Christ and be found in him, not having a righteousness of my own that comes from the law, but that which comes through faith in Christ, the righteousness from God that depends on faith—that I may know him and the power of his resurrection, and may share his sufferings, becoming like him in his death, that by any means possible I may attain the resurrection from the dead.
>
> —PHILIPPIANS 3:8–11

In other words, Paul did not hide behind any sense of academic detachment from the doctrines he so powerfully taught. Nor did he set before his congregation in Philippi a series of alternate renderings of doctrine. Instead, he taught clearly, defended his case, and made clear that he embraced these very doctrines as the substance of his life and faith.

Of course, the experiential nature of the pastor's confession does not at all imply that the authority for theology lies in personal experience. To the contrary, the authority must always remain the Word of God. But the experiential character of the pastor's theological calling is not unimportant. It underlines the fact that the preacher is speaking from within the circle of faith as a passionate and committed believer, not from a position of detachment as a mere observer. Further, the pastor's confession of his faith and personal example add both authority and authenticity to the pastoral ministry. Without these, the pastor can end up sounding more like a theological consultant than a faithful shepherd. The congregation must be able to observe the pastor basing his life and ministry upon these truths, not merely teaching them in the pulpit.

In the end, every preacher stands under the same mandate that Paul handed down to Timothy: "Follow the pattern of the sound words that you have heard from me, in the faith and love that are in Christ Jesus. By the Holy Spirit who dwells within us, guard the good deposit entrusted to you" (2 Timothy 1:13–14). In other words, we are the stewards of sound words and the guardians of doctrinal treasure that has been entrusted to us at the very core of our calling as pastors. The pastor who is no theologian is no pastor.

CHAPTER 8

STRANGER THAN IT USED TO BE

Preaching to a Postmodern Culture

Acommon concern seems to emerge now wherever Christians gather: The task of truth-telling is stranger than it used to be. In this age, telling the truth is tough business and not for the faint-hearted. The times are increasingly strange. That sense of strangeness is at least partly due to the rise of postmodern culture and philosophy, perhaps the most important intellectual and cultural movement of the late twentieth century. What difference does post-modernism make? Just look at the modern media and pop culture, or consider the blank stares you receive from some persons when you talk about truth, meaning, and morality.

Postmodernism first developed among academics and artists, but it has quickly spread throughout the culture. At the most basic level, postmodernism refers to the passing of modernity and the rise of a new cultural movement. Modernity, the dominant worldview since the Enlightenment, has been supplanted by *post*modernism, which extends certain principles and symbols central to the modern age, even as it denies others.

Much of the literature of postmodernism is nonsensical and hard to take seriously. When major postmodern figures speak or write, the gibberish that often results sounds more like a vocabulary test than a sustained argument. But postmodernism cannot be dismissed as unimportant or irrelevant. This is a matter of concern not only among academics and the avant-garde. This new movement represents a critical challenge to the Christian church and to the individual Christian.

Actually, postmodernism may not be a movement or methodology at all. We might best describe postmodernism as a mood that sets itself apart from the certainties of the modern age. This mood is the heart of the postmodern challenge. What are the contours of this postmodern mood? Is this new movement helpful in our presentation of the gospel? Or, will the postmodern age bring a great retreat from Christian truth? A look at the basic features of postmodernism may be helpful.

THE POSTMODERN TERRAIN:
THE DECONSTRUCTION OF TRUTH

Though the nature of truth has been debated throughout the centuries, postmodernism has turned this debate on its head. While most arguments throughout history have focused on rival claims to truth, postmodernism rejects the very notion of truth as fixed, universal, objective, or absolute.

Postmodernists argue that truth is socially constructed, plural, and inaccessible to universal reason.

The Christian tradition understands truth as established by God and known to us through the self-revelation of God in Scripture. Truth is eternal, fixed, and universal, and our responsibility is to order our minds in accordance with God's revealed truth and then to bear witness to this truth. We serve a Savior who identified Himself as "the Way, the Truth, and the Life" (see John 14:6) and called for belief.

Modern science, itself a product of the Enlightenment, rejected revelation as a source of truth and put the scientific method in its place. Modernity attempted to establish truth on the basis of scientific precision through the process of inductive thought and investigation. Following the lead of scientists, other disciplines attempted also to establish objective truth through rational thought. Modernists were confident that their approach would yield objective and universal truths by means of human reason.

Postmodernists reject both the Christian and modernist approaches to the question of truth. According to postmodern theory, truth is not universal, is not objective or absolute, and cannot be determined by a commonly accepted method. Instead, postmodernists argue that truth is relative, plural, and inaccessible to universal reason. As postmodern philosopher Richard Rorty asserts, truth is *made* rather than *found*. According to the deconstructionists, one influential sect among postmodernists, all truth is socially constructed. That is, social groups construct their own "truth" in order to serve their own interests, but what is "true" for one group is not necessarily "true" for any other.

Michel Foucault, one of the most significant postmodern theorists, argued that all claims to truth are constructed to serve those in power. Thus, the role of the intellectual is to deconstruct truth claims in order to liberate the society. So what has been understood and affirmed as truth, argue the postmodernists, is really nothing more than a convenient structure of thought intended to oppress the powerless.

Truth is not universal, for every culture establishes its own truth. Nor is truth objectively real, for all truth is merely constructed. In other words, it is made, not found.

Little imagination is needed to see that this radical relativism is a direct challenge to the Christian gospel. Our claim is not to preach one truth among many, one Savior among many, or one gospel among many. We do not believe that the Christian gospel is a socially constructed truth but the Truth that sets sinners free from sin—and is objectively, universally, historically true. As the late Francis Schaeffer instructed, the Christian church must contend for "true truth."

THE POSTMODERN TERRAIN:
THE DEATH OF THE METANARRATIVE

Since postmodernists believe all truth to be socially constructed, all presentations of absolute, universal, established truth must be resisted. Thus all grand and expansive accounts of truth, meaning, and existence are cast aside as "metanarratives" that claim far more than they can deliver.

It was Jean-Francois Lyotard, as we have seen, who defined postmodernism as "incredulity toward metanarratives."[1] Thus, all the great philosophical systems are dead, all cultural accounts are limited, and all that remains are little stories accepted as true by different groups and cultures. Claims to universal truth—the metanarratives—are oppressive and "totalizing," and thus they must be resisted.

The problem with this, of course, is that Christianity is meaningless apart from the gospel—which is most certainly a metanarrative. Indeed, the Christian gospel is nothing less than the Metanarrative of all metanarratives. For Christianity to surrender the claim that the gospel is universally true and objectively established is to surrender the center of our faith. Christianity is the great metanarrative of redemption. Our story begins with creation by the sovereign, omnipotent God, continues through the fall of humanity into sin and the redemption of sinners through the substitutionary work of Christ on the cross, and promises finally an eternal destiny for all humanity—the redeemed with God forever in glory and the unredeemed in eternal punishment. That is the message we bear, and it is a life-transforming and world-changing metanarrative.

As Christians, we do not present the gospel as one narrative among many true narratives or merely as "our" narrative alongside the authentic narratives of others. We cannot retreat to claim that biblical truth is merely true for us. Our claim is that the Bible is the Word of God for all—a claim that is deeply offensive to the postmodern worldview, which charges all who claim universal truth with imperialism and oppression.

The rise of postmodernism presents Christians with the undeniable reality that many people simply do not accept the idea that truth is absolute, or even that written texts have a fixed meaning. All claims to truth—especially claims to universally valid truth—are met with suspicion, or worse. This presents the Christian with a changed climate for truth-telling and a genuine intellectual challenge.

THE POSTMODERN TERRAIN: THE DEMISE OF THE TEXT

If the metanarrative is dead, then the great texts behind the metanarratives must also be dead. Postmodernism asserts that it is a fallacy to ascribe any meaning to a text or even to the text's author. It is the reader, postmodernists say, who establishes the meaning, and there are no controls that limit the meaning that can be imposed.

The late Jacques Derrida, a leading literary deconstructionist, described this move in terms of the "death of the author" and the "death of the text."[2] Meaning is created by the reader in the act of reading. Indeed the text must be deconstructed in order to get rid of the author and

> In the name of postmodernism, anything can be explained away as a matter of interpretation.

let the text live as a liberating word. This new hermeneutical method explains much of the current debate in literature, politics, law, and theology. All texts—whether the Holy Scripture, the United States Constitution, or the works of Mark Twain—are subjected to esoteric criticism and dissection, all in the name of liberation. Every text, according to the postmodernists, reveals a subtext of oppressive intentions on the part of the author, and so must be deconstructed. This is no matter of mere academic significance. This is the argument behind much contemporary constitutional interpretation made by judges, the presentation of issues in the media, and the fragmentation of modern biblical scholarship. The rise of feminist, liberation, homosexual, and various other interest-group schools of interpretation is central to this postmodern principle.

The Bible too is subjected to radical reinterpretation, often with little or no regard for the plain meaning of the text or the clear intention of the human author. Texts that are not pleasing to the postmodern mind are rejected as oppressive, patriarchal, heterosexist, homophobic, or deformed by some other political or ideological bias. The authority of the text is denied in the name of liberation, and the most fanciful and ridiculous interpretations are celebrated as "affirming" and thus "authentic."

Gene Veith, dean of the school of arts and sciences at Concordia University, tells of a young man who claimed to be a Christian and professed belief in Christ and love for the Bible, but who also believed in reincarnation. His pastor confronted this belief in reincarnation by directing the young man to Hebrews 9:27 (NASB). The text was read: "It is appointed for men to die once and after that comes judgment." The young man looked back at his pastor and replied, "Well, that's your interpretation." The young man was simply unwilling to be instructed and bound by the biblical text. In the name of postmodernism, anything can be explained away as a matter of interpretation.

Of course, the notion of the "death of the author" takes on an entirely new meaning when applied to Scripture, for we claim that the Bible is not the mere words of men but the Word of God. Postmodernism's insistence on the death of the author is inherently anti-supernaturalistic and ultimately atheistic. The claim to divine revelation is written off as only one more projection of oppressive power that must be resisted.

THE POSTMODERN TERRAIN:
THE DOMINION OF THERAPY

When truth is denied, therapy remains. The critical question shifts from "What is true?" to "What makes me feel good?" This cultural trend has been developing during past decades, but has reached epic proportions in the last few years.

The culture we confront is almost completely under submission to what Philip Reiff called the "triumph of the therapeutic." In a post-modern world, all issues eventually revolve around the self. Thus, enhanced self-esteem is all that remains as the goal of many educational and theological approaches, with categories such as "sin" rejected as oppressive and harmful to self-esteem. Therapeutic approaches are dominant in a postmodern culture made up of individuals uncertain that truth even exists, but quite assured that our self-esteem must remain intact. Right and wrong are discarded as out-of-date reminders of an oppressive past. In the name of our own "authenticity," we will reject all inconvenient moral standards and replace concern for right and wrong with the assertion of our rights.

Theology is likewise reduced to therapy. Entire theological systems and approaches are constructed with the goal reduced to nothing more than self-esteem for individuals and special groups. These "feel good" theologies dispense with the "negativity" of offensive biblical texts or even with the Bible altogether. Out are categories such as "lostness" and judgment, and in their place are erected notions of acceptance without repentance and wholeness without redemption. We may not know (or care) if we are saved or lost, but we certainly do feel better about ourselves.

THE POSTMODERN TERRAIN:
THE DECLINE OF AUTHORITY

Because postmodern culture is committed to a radical vision of liberation, all authorities must be overthrown, including texts, authors, traditions, metanarratives, the Bible, God, and all powers on heaven and earth. All authority is denounced, deconstructed, and cast aside— except, of course, for the authority of the postmodern theorists and cultural figures themselves, who wield their power in the name of oppressed peoples everywhere.

According to the postmodernists, those in authority use their power to remain in power, and to serve their own interests. Their laws, traditions, texts, and "truth" are nothing more than that which is designed to keep them in power. So the authority of governmental leaders is eroded, along with the authority of teachers, community leaders, parents, and ministers. Ultimately, even the authority of God is rejected as totalitarian and autocratic. Christians—especially Christian ministers—are seen as representatives of this autocratic deity, and are to be resisted as authorities as well. Doctrines, traditions, creeds, and confessions—all these are to be rejected and charged with limiting self-expression and representing oppressive authority. Preachers are tolerated so long as they stick to therapeutic messages of enhanced self-esteem, but are resisted whenever they inject divine authority or universal claims to truth in their sermons.

THE POSTMODERN TERRAIN:
THE DISPLACEMENT OF MORALITY

Ivan in Fyodor Dostoyevsky's novel *The Brothers Karamazov* was right—if God is dead, everything is permissible. The God allowed by postmodernism is not the God of the Bible but a vague concept of spirituality. There are no tablets of stone, no Ten Commandments . . . no rules.

Morality, along with other foundations of culture, is discarded by postmodernists as oppressive and totalitarian. A pervasive moral relativism marks postmodern culture. This is not to say that postmodernists are reluctant to employ moral language. To the contrary, postmodern culture is filled with moral discourse. But the issues of moral concern are quite arbitrary, and in many cases represent a reversal of biblical morality. Take the issue of homosexuality, for example. The rise of gay and lesbian studies in universities, the emergence of homosexual political power, and the homoerotic images now common to popular culture mark a dramatic moral reversal. Homosexuality is no longer considered a sin. It is "homophobia" that is now targeted as the real sin, and demands for tolerance of "alternative lifestyles" have morphed into demands for public *celebration* of all lifestyles as morally equal.

> The task of preaching must be understood as an apologetic calling.

Michael Jones has described modernity as "rationalized sexual misbehavior,"[3] and postmodernity is its logical extension. Foucault, who argued that all sexual morality is an abuse of power, called for postmodernism to celebrate the concept of perversity. He lived and died dedicated to this lifestyle, and his prophecy has been fulfilled in this decade. The very idea of perversity has become perverse to the postmodern culture. Everything is permitted.

RESPONDING TO THE CHALLENGE OF POSTMODERNISM

How should we approach the task of preaching in the face of such confusion? In an age when the reality of truth is itself denied, when most persons think their most basic problems are rooted in a lack of self-esteem, and when personal choice is the all-determining reality of the marketplace, how should we go about proclaiming and defending a gospel that declares to people that they are sinners in need of the one and only Savior?

I would argue that at this critical time of cultural and intellectual transition, the task of preaching must be understood as an apologetic calling. Apologetics—the task of setting forth the truth claims of Christianity and arguing for the unique truthfulness of the Christian faith—

must inform every preacher's understanding of his task in a postmodern age.

In Acts 17:16–34, we find a model of Great Commission proclamation matched to an apologetic argument—an argument in defense of Christian truth. In that passage, we find Paul standing at the center of apologetic ministry in the first century—Athens. Athens was the most intellectually sophisticated culture in the ancient world, and even in Paul's day it basked in its retreating glory. Though Rome held political and military preeminence, Athens stood supreme in terms of cultural and intellectual influence. The centerpiece of Paul's visit to Athens is his message to the court of philosophers at the Areopagus, also known as Mars Hill. Some critics have claimed that Paul's experience on Mars Hill was a dismal failure. Luke presents it otherwise, however, and in this account we can learn a great deal about the proper proclamation of the gospel and defense of the faith. Several principles become evident as we consider this great biblical text.

First, Christian proclamation in a postmodern culture begins in a provoked spirit (Acts 17:16). Paul observed the spiritual confusion of the Athenians and was overcome with concern. The sight of a city full of idols seized him with grief, and that grief turned to gospel proclamation. Luke records that Paul experienced *paroxysmos*, a paroxysm, at the sight of such spiritual confusion. Athens was intellectually sophisticated—the arena where the ancient world's most famous philosophers had debated. This was the city of Pericles, Plato, and Socrates. But Paul was not impressed with the faded glory. He saw men and women in need of a Savior.

This text reminds us that a proper Christian apologetic begins in spiritual concern, not in intellectual snobbery or scorn. We preach Christ not because Christianity is merely a superior philosophy or worldview, nor because we have been smart enough to embrace the gospel, but because we have met the Savior, we have been claimed by the gospel, and we have been transformed by the renewing of our minds. Our preaching is not a matter of intellectual pride but of spiritual concern. A dying world languishes in spiritual confusion. I wonder how many of us are as grieved by that as Paul was in his observation of Athens. Looking at the spiritual confusion of American culture, do we experience the paroxysm with which Paul was seized?

We live in a nation filled with idols of self-realization, material comfort, psychological salvation, sexual ecstasy, ambition, power, and success. Millions of Americans embrace New Age spiritualities in a quest for personal fulfillment and self-transcendence. The ancient paganisms of nature worship have emerged once again, along with esoteric and occult practices. As journalist Walter Truett Anderson observes,

> Never before has any civilization made available to its populace such a smorgasbord of realities. Never before has a communications system like the contemporary mass media made information about religion—all religions—available to so many people. Never has a society allowed its people to become consumers of belief, and allowed belief—all beliefs—to become merchandise.[4]

America, he says, has become the "belief basket of the world."

I fear that we have become too acculturated, too blind, and too unimpressed with the paganisms and idolatries all around us. We betray a comfort level that Paul would see as scandalous. Where is the gripping realization that millions of men and women are slaves to the idols of our age? Where is the courage to confront the idols on their own ground?

Second, Christian proclamation in a postmodern culture is focused on gospel proclamation (Acts 17:17). Moved by the city full of idols, Paul went to the synagogue and to the marketplace each day, presenting the claims of Christ and reasoning with both Jews and Gentiles. The goal of apologetic preaching is not to win an argument but to win souls. Apologetics separated from evangelism is unknown in the New Testament, and it is clearly foreign to the model offered by the apostle Paul. The great missionary was about the business of preaching the gospel, presenting the claims of Christ, and calling for men and women to believe in the Lord Jesus Christ and be saved.

For too many evangelicals, the study of apologetics is reduced to philosophical structures and rational arguments. This is not Paul's method. He is not merely concerned with the justification of truth claims, but more profoundly he is concerned for the justification of sinners. This is another reminder of the fact that every true theologian is an evangelist, and every true evangelist is a theologian. The gospel possesses content and presents truth claims that demand our keenest arguments

Large numbers of Americans . . . profess belief in God but live like atheists.

and boldest proclamation. But Christianity is not merely a truth to be affirmed. It is a gospel to be received. Moved by the sight of idols, Paul preached Christ, and called for belief.

Third, Christian proclamation in a postmodern culture assumes a context of spiritual confusion (Acts 17:18–21). Paul's gospel proclamation brought confusion to the Athenian intellectuals. The Epicureans, the forerunners of modern secularists, and the Stoics, committed to pantheistic rationalism, accused Paul of teaching nonsense.

Confusion marks the spiritual understanding of most Americans. Pollsters report amazingly large numbers of Americans who profess belief in God but live like atheists. The vast majority of Americans profess to be Christians but have no concept of Christian belief or discipleship. A quick look around the local trade bookshop will reveal something of the contours of America's spiritual confusion. Books on religion and spirituality abound, but most are empty of content. You know you are in a confused age when a popular book is entitled *That's Funny, You Don't Look Buddhist: On Being a Faithful Jew and a Passionate Buddhist.* Sadly, this confusion has invaded our churches as well. An amazing number of Christians allow for belief in reincarnation, channeling, or other spiritualist manifestations.

To the Athenians—and to modern secular Americans—the preaching of the authentic gospel sounds strange. "You are bringing some strange things to our ears," the Athenians responded to Paul. The Christian preacher hears this same response today. In postmodern America, the Christian gospel is strange in its whole and in its parts. Most Americans assume themselves to be good and decent persons, and they are amused at the notion that they are sinners against God. Grace, too, is an alien concept in American culture. Sin is almost outlawed as a category, substitutionary atonement sounds unfair, and God in human flesh is too much to take. Yet that is what we preach.

The Athenians and their tourists loved to spend their time telling or hearing something new—but what Paul preached was simply too much. Americans today are like the Athenians in more ways than they know. Consumers of meaning just as much as they are of cars and clothing, Americans will test-drive new spiritualities and try on a whole series of lifestyles. To many, the gospel is just too strange, too countercultural, too propositional, and too exclusive. To contend for the gospel and biblical morality in this culture is to run the risk of being cited for "hate speech." We must assume a context of spiritual confusion, and this is often now a hostile confusion. The gospel sounds not only strange but threatening to the local deities.

> We must assume a context of spiritual confusion, and this is often now a hostile confusion.

Fourth, Christian proclamation in a postmodern culture is directed to a spiritual hunger (Acts 17:22–23). Paul's observation convinced him that the Athenians were a religious people. A deficit of religiosity was not the problem. In fact, judging from the statue Paul noticed, the Athenians seemed to be fearful lest they miss any new philosophy or neglect any unknown deity.

American culture is increasingly secularistic. The past century has seen the agenda of secularism accomplished in the courts, in the schools, in the marketplace, and in the media. And yet Americans are among the most religious people in the world. The emptiness of the secular wasteland haunts most postmodern persons. They long for something more. Many people declare themselves to live by scientific rationality, and yet they read the astrology charts, believe in alien abductions, line up to see bleeding statues, and talk about past lives. In America, even some atheists say they believe in miracles. Sociologist Robert Wuthnow suggests that "Americans are particularly fascinated with miraculous manifestations of the sacred because they are uncertain whether the sacred has really gone away."[5]

Paul had taken account of the plentiful idols and houses of worship found in Athens. He even noted that they were hedging their bets, lest they offend some deity who had not made himself known. Paul seized the opportunity. Brought before the court at the Areopagus, he referred to the altar he had seen that was dedicated to an unknown god. "It just so happens," he asserted, "that I know that God. Therefore what you worship in ignorance, this I proclaim to you."

This is surely a pattern for Christian preaching in a postmodern age. We must seek constantly to turn spiritual hunger toward the true food of the gospel of Christ. God has placed that hunger within lost persons so that they might desire Christ. We bear the stewardship of proclaiming the gospel, and therefore we must muster the courage to confront confused postmodernists with the reality of their spiritual ignorance. Paul never allowed this ignorance to become an excuse, but there can be no doubt that it is a reality. Americans, too, are feeding on a false diet of superstition and myths. The hunger is a place to start. Our challenge is to preach Christ as the only answer to that hunger.

Fifth, Christian proclamation in a postmodern culture begins with the fundamental issue of God's nature, character, power, and authority (Acts 17:24–28). Interestingly, Paul does not begin with Christ and the cross but with the knowledge of God in creation. The God who created the world is not looking for Corinthian columns and the Parthenon, Paul argued. He does not dwell in temples made with human hands. He is the author of life itself, and He needs nothing from us. Furthermore, He has made humanity and is Lord over all the nations. He sovereignly determines their times and boundaries. The Athenians were partly right, said Paul, quoting their poets. All human beings are God's children, but not in the sense the Athenians believed. In proclaiming God as the Creator, Ruler, and Sustainer of all things and all peoples, Paul was making a claim that far surpassed the claims of the Hellenistic deities.

Paul established his preaching of Christ upon the larger foundation of the knowledge of the God of the Bible, Maker of heaven and earth. That is also how we must structure our own proclamation of the gospel in this postmodern age. People must first understand God the Creator before they will understand God the Redeemer. John Calvin organized his systematic theology around what he called the *duplex cognito Domini*, the twofold knowledge of God. We must start with the knowledge of God as Creator, but this is not sufficient to save. "It is one thing to feel that God our Maker supports us by his power, governs us by his providence, nourishes us by his goodness, and attends us with all sorts of blessings," Calvin said, "and another thing to embrace the reconciliation offered us in Christ."[6] Seeing people come to faith in Christ the Redeemer begins with seeing them come to grips with the fact that God is their Maker.

> Error must be confronted, heresy must be opposed, and false teachings must be corrected.

Sixth, Christian proclamation in a postmodern culture confronts error (Acts 17:29). In this sense, preaching, apologetics, and polemics are all related. Error must be confronted, heresy must be opposed, and false teachings must be corrected. Paul was bold to correct the Athenians with a firm injunction: We ought not to think false thoughts about God. The Athenians made idols out of marble and precious metals. Paul rebuked this practice and proclaimed that the Divine Nature is not like gold or silver or stone. Furthermore, God is not "an image formed by the art and thought of man."

False theologies abound no less in the postmodern marketplace of ideas. Americans have revived old heresies and invented new ones. Mormons believe that God is a celestial being with a sex partner. The ecological mystics believe that the world is God—the so-called Gaia Hypothesis. New Age devotees believe that God is infinite empowerment. Our culture is filled with images of gods formed by art and the thought of man. Our confrontation must be bold and biblical. We have no right to make God in our image.

Seventh, Christian proclamation in a postmodern culture affirms the totality of God's saving purpose (Acts 17:30–31). Paul brought his presentation of the gospel to a climactic conclusion by calling for repentance and warning of the judgment that is to come. He proclaimed Christ as the appointed Savior who will judge the world and whose identity has been clearly revealed by the fact that God has raised Him from the dead.

It is not enough to preach Christ without calling for belief and repentance. It is not enough to promise the blessings of heaven without warning of the threat of hell. It is not enough to preach salvation without pointing to judgment.

Authentic Christian preaching both declares and defends the whole gospel. The center of our proclamation is Jesus Christ the Savior, who was crucified for sinners, was raised by the power of God, is coming again in glory and in judgment, and is even now sitting and ruling at the right hand of God the Father Almighty. We must defend the truths of Christ's deity, the virgin birth, the historicity of the miracles, the truth of the incarnation, the reality of His substitutionary death, and the assurance of His bodily resurrection. Yet we dare not stop at these affirmations, for we must place the person and work of Christ within the context of God's eternal purpose to save a people to His own glory and to exalt Himself among the nations. The task of preaching in this postmodern context is comprehensive, even as it is driven by the desire to see sinners turn to Christ in faith.

The postmodern world has no need of half evangelists preaching a half gospel to the half converted, and leading a halfhearted church. What is needed is a generation of bold and courageous preacher-apologists for the twenty-first century—men who will be witnesses to the whole world of the power of the gospel and who will proclaim the whole counsel of God.

CHAPTER 9

THE URGENCY OF PREACHING

An Exhortation to Preachers

The Puritan Richard Baxter once remarked, "I preach'd as never sure to preach again. I preach'd as a dying man to dying men."[1]

Every generation of preachers is confronted with a new set of challenges, both intellectual and spiritual. For Baxter, that challenge was a world still settling itself after the upheaval of the Reformation and just beginning to experience the intellectual revolution of the Enlightenment. For us, the challenge is somewhat different—a postmodern world in which truth has been deconstructed, therapy reigns, authority and texts have been discarded, and morality has been displaced in favor of therapeutic ways of thought. But even as we face different challenges in a different age, the world's need to hear the gospel of Jesus Christ is just as urgent today as it was in Baxter's day— or Luther's, or Augustine's, or Paul's. The challenges we face may be different, but the sense of urgency in our preaching cannot be. Each of us must preach as a dying man to dying men.

As in so many other ways, the apostle Paul provides us with a model for the kind of urgency that is to mark Christian preachers. Perhaps nowhere is this clearer than in his letter to the church at Rome. As many Christians have pointed out through the centuries, the book of Romans is a majestic exposition of the gospel of Jesus Christ. Yet this is an exposition of the gospel that pulses with urgency. Paul is not laying an idea out for people's "careful consideration." He is preaching a message that means the difference between life and death.

WHY WE PREACH WITH URGENCY . . .

I see in the book of Romans at least three reasons why Paul preached with such a sense of urgency: First, because sinners desperately need to be saved; second, because this gospel we preach is the only way of salvation; and third, because sinners will not hear and will not believe unless we preach to them.

. . . BECAUSE SINNERS DESPERATELY NEED TO BE SAVED

In the very first chapter of Romans, Paul explains why the need of people for the gospel is so great. It is because they are under the wrath of God: "For the wrath of God is revealed from heaven against all ungodliness and unrighteousness of men, who by their unrighteousness suppress the truth" (Romans 1:18).

> The Bible defines God's wrath as His settled opposition to sin.

With that statement, Paul takes us onto some of the most politically incorrect terrain in the entire New Testament—the wrath of God. If there is any one Christian doctrine that is most uniformly dismissed by a post-Christian, postmodern world, this is it. So repulsive is the idea of God's wrath, in fact, that many churches and theologians have tried to deny it altogether. "To say that God has wrath is a misunderstanding," they say. "Sin is not really the issue. God is more like an indulgent grandfather who just wants His grandchildren to get along with one another. There is no wrath, or if there is, it is nothing more than the natural consequences of our selfish actions. But God does not respond with wrath." If that is the case, then the urgency of the gospel is lessened considerably. But it most certainly is not the case, and those who argue that God does not respond to sinful humanity with wrath should read the Bible more carefully. The gospel of Jesus Christ reveals to us the wrath of God.

Part of the problem is that we tend to anthropomorphize God, to make Him too much like us and to project our shortcomings onto Him. Thus we recoil at the idea of God being "wrathful." You see, when we experience wrath, it is usually something that just swells up within us. Sometimes it is righteous indignation; sometimes it is unrighteous anger. But either way, it is an emotional response that is occasioned in us by some unexpected event. God's wrath is different. The Bible defines God's wrath as His settled opposition to sin. That means His wrath is not something that simply welled up within Him after He observed human sin. It is rather a consistent manifestation of His holy character, a settled determination that He must and will punish sin.

To many in our day, the idea that God would punish sin is as foreign as the idea that He would be wrathful. For most people, sin is not even a category anymore, and when the word is used—whether in advertising or literature or music—it most often means something like "fun that you really don't want anyone to know you're having." But Paul could not be clearer in describing the nature and effects of human sin, and the picture he paints is grotesque:

> For although they knew God, they did not honor him as God or give thanks to him, but they became futile in their thinking, and their foolish hearts were darkened. Claiming to be wise, they became fools, and exchanged the glory of the immortal God for images resembling

mortal man and birds and animals and reptiles. Therefore God gave them up in the lusts of their hearts to impurity, to the dishonoring of their bodies among themselves, because they exchanged the truth about God for a lie and worshiped and served the creature rather than the Creator, who is blessed forever! Amen. For this reason God gave them up to dishonorable passions. For their women exchanged natural relations for those that are contrary to nature; and the men likewise gave up natural relations with women and were consumed with passion for one another, men committing shameless acts with men and receiving in themselves the due penalty for their error. And since they did not see fit to acknowledge God, God gave them up to a debased mind to do what ought not to be done.

—ROMANS 1:21–28

Notice how Paul describes humanity's sin and rebellion against God as a series of insane exchanges. "They *exchanged* the glory of the immoral God for images resembling mortal man and birds and animals and reptiles" (verse 23). They "*exchanged* the truth about God for a lie" (verse 25). And then in verse 26, the "women *exchanged* natural relations for those that are contrary to nature." What we see here is the utter sinfulness of sin. Faced with the choice between obedience and disobedience, we choose to disobey. Confronted with a choice between the one true and living God or the idols, we choose the idols. Forced to choose between submission to the authority of God and ridiculous claims to our own personal autonomy, we choose personal autonomy.

Paul points in this passage to the corruption of human sexuality as a primary manifestation of humanity's rebellion against God. What he describes, very graphically, clearly, and honestly, is a pattern of sexual perversion. Both women and men exchange the sexual order God intended in favor of a perverse, burning lust for those of the same sex. But sexual perversion is only the beginning, because Paul's point is broader than simply affirming the sinfulness of homosexuality— though he unquestionably does so here. His aim is to charge every human being in the world with sin, to point out that sin and rebellion is not the story of just some of humanity but of all. Men and women alike have "all manner of unrighteousness, evil, covetousness, malice." Then he names their sins: "envy, murder, strife, deceit, maliciousness. They are gossips, slanderers, haters of God, insolent, haughty, boastful, inventors of evil, disobedient to parents, foolish, faithless, heartless, ruthless" (Romans 1:29–31).

Not one of us escapes that verdict. Every last one of us is charged, arrested, indicted, and convicted of our rebellion against God. As Paul says a couple of chapters later, "For all have sinned and fall short of the glory of God" (Romans 3:23).

When God's judgment falls, there will be no excuse for anyone. Paul said it clearly in Romans 1:19–20: "For what can be known about God is plain to them, because God has shown it to them. For his invisible attributes, namely, his eternal power and divine nature, have been clearly perceived, ever since the creation of the world, in the things that have been made. So they are without excuse." On the day of judgment, no one will be able to say, "I didn't know there was a God," or, "I didn't know what You required of me." There will be no plea bargain or defense. Every mouth will be closed, every tongue will be stopped, and the whole world will be held accountable to God.

> Time is short, God's wrath is certain, and eternity hangs in the balance.

Every so often I hear someone remark, "You know, I am tired of all this preaching about sin and judgment and hell." Frankly, I would like to know where these people are going to church, because I find that kind of biblical preaching far too rare. In all too many pulpits, God has become our next-door neighbor, our great cosmic companion, or the divine leader of our small group, rather than the holy God of Abraham, Isaac, and Jacob. Perhaps the lack of urgency in so much preaching today comes from a lack of understanding about humanity's awful predicament. The greatest problem we human beings face is not a shortage of self-esteem. It is that we have rebelled against God, and, in His holiness, God will one day hold us to horrible account for our sin.

The gospel necessarily comes with an urgent warning, because the distinction between those who obey its call and those who disobey is not merely between a better life and a worse life. It is the difference between life and death. It is an eternal distinction, for the cost of disobedience and the cost of not hearing the gospel is eternal death.

That is why we must preach with the urgency of a dying man. It is because human beings are in desperate need of salvation. Time is short, God's wrath is certain, and eternity hangs in the balance. Moreover, there is for each of us only one way out of this predicament, and that is the salvation God Himself has won through the gospel of His Son, Jesus Christ.

. . . BECAUSE THE GOSPEL SAVES

At the very beginning of Romans, Paul makes a statement that shows us why he was willing to endure so much for the sake of the gospel. It also provides another reason for why our preaching ought never to be marked by a sense of apathy or indifference. "I am not ashamed of the gospel," declared Paul, "for it is the power of God for salvation to everyone who believes, to the Jew first and also to the Greek" (Romans 1:16).

Paul is not ashamed of this gospel he preaches because it—and it alone—is the gospel that saves. There is no other way of salvation. At the very center of Jesus' Great Commission to the church, at the very center of our call to preach the gospel to the world, is the understanding that there is only one message that saves. There is only one Savior. Humanity can be divided in so many different ways—by ethnicity, language, educational and economic levels—but the one division that will matter eternally is the division between those who know Christ and those who do not.

In the next verse (Romans 1:17), Paul gives a short description of how the gospel saves. It is a theme that he will unpack for the rest of the book: "For in it [the gospel] the righteousness of God is revealed from faith for faith, as it is written, 'The righteous shall live by faith.'" When Paul talks about "the righteousness of God," we must always keep in mind that he means by that phrase two things. First, the phrase "righteousness of God" refers to God's own righteousness— His absolutely perfect and unalloyed righteousness. God is not righteous because He measures up well against some external standard of right and wrong. He is righteous in His very nature, which means that we know what righteousness is—what is right and what is wrong —only because the one true and living God has revealed His character to us.

Second, Paul means by "the righteousness of God" the righteousness that is imputed, or credited, to the believer in Jesus Christ. The great question of the gospel is how God can deal with sinful human beings without compromising His own perfect righteousness. One way, of course, is to pour out His wrath on us, to rightly punish us for our rebellion against Him. But is that the only way? Is there any way that God can forgive our sin without becoming complicit in our evil?

In answer to that great question, the apostle points us to the cross of the Lord Jesus. "But now the righteousness of God has been manifested apart from the law," Paul writes.

> Although the Law and the Prophets bear witness to it—the righteousness of God through faith in Jesus Christ for all who believe. For there is no distinction: for all have sinned and fall short of the glory of God, and are justified by his grace as a gift, through the redemption that is in Christ Jesus, whom God put forward as a propitiation by his blood, to be received by faith. This was to show God's righteousness, because in his divine forbearance he had passed over former sins. It was to show his righteousness at the present time, so that he might be just and the justifier of the one who has faith in Jesus.
>
> —Romans 3:21–26

The glory of the Christian gospel is that God not only demanded that sacrifice, but He provided it as well.

What Paul teaches in this incredible passage is that the way God could forgive our sin without compromising His righteousness was by accepting His own Son's death as a full and final sacrifice for our sin. The phrase "propitiation" in verse 25 refers to a sacrifice of atonement. That is what God demanded in payment for sin—a full and infinite sacrifice that would be equivalent to the infinite insult to His holiness and glory that is represented by human sin.

So how could God forgive sin without violating His own righteousness? By demanding a sacrifice that would be equal to the insult of sin.

Yet the glory of the Christian gospel is that God not only demanded that sacrifice, but He provided it as well. "God put [Jesus] forward," Paul says, "as a propitiation by his blood, to be received by faith." God demanded a sacrifice, and God provided that sacrifice in the person of Jesus Christ. Dying on the cross, Jesus paid the demanded penalty for the sins of all the redeemed, so that God's righteousness might be revealed, and He might be simultaneously "just and the justifier of the one who has faith in Jesus." You see, there is only one message that explains how that could possibly be, and that is the good news of the incarnation, death, burial, and resurrection of the Lord Jesus Christ. No wonder Paul said he was not ashamed of this gospel!

But the beauty of the gospel story is not the only reason that Paul preaches with such urgency. It is also that he is truly convinced that this gospel does what it claims—it saves! The apostle writes this in Romans 10 as he explains the pressing obligation of the Jews to believe in Christ:

But what does it say? "The word is near you, in your mouth and in your heart" (that is, the word of faith that we proclaim); because, if you confess with your mouth that Jesus is Lord and believe in your heart that God raised him from the dead, you will be saved. For with the heart one believes and is justified, and with the mouth one confesses and is saved. For the Scripture says, "Everyone who believes in him will not be put to shame." For there is no distinction between Jew and Greek; the same Lord is Lord of all, bestowing his riches on all who call on him. For "everyone who calls on the name of the Lord will be saved." But how are they to call on him in whom they have not believed? And how are they to believe in him of whom they have never heard? And how are they to hear without someone preaching?

—ROMANS 10:8–14

This gospel of Jesus Christ, Paul asserts, is a message that comes with a promise. "If you confess with your mouth that Jesus is Lord and believe in your heart that God raised him from the dead, you will be saved." This is not just a hope; it is an assured promise. Everyone who calls upon the name of the Lord *will* be saved. That passage means just what it says. It means that everyone who responds to the word of the gospel with faith will be saved.

This promise is what fires our confidence in preaching the gospel. Can you imagine what we would have to say if we did not have this truth? "There is a fairly good likelihood that if you believe, you'll be saved." Or, "You'll just have to take your chances—but it's a good bet!" There are none of those games or equivocations here—nothing but the simple and direct promise of God. If you believe, you will be saved.

Even more, this is not a promise that is made to just some. It is a universal promise, that *everyone* who believes will be saved. That was a difficult idea for some Christians in the Roman church to grasp. They could easily understand how the promise of salvation could be given to the Jews. After all, they were the people of God—the nation God had rescued from Egypt, given the law, and led into the land of promise. The problem was that they believed the promise of salvation was for them alone, and that is exactly the idea that Paul is laboring to refute. "There is no distinction," he insists, "between Jew and Greek; the same Lord is Lord of all, bestowing his riches on all who call on him" (Romans 10:12). The gospel of Jesus Christ is for everyone. Both Jews and Gentiles are equally in need of salvation, and the promise of the gospel is offered to both.

Just as it was difficult for some in the first-century church to understand that idea, so it is difficult for some in our own day to grasp it. That is why we need frequently to remind ourselves of that glorious picture in the book of Revelation of people from every tongue, tribe, people, and nation standing before the throne of God. Our God loves languages, and the fact that humanity consists of many different cultures reflects God's desire to be worshiped in many tongues and in many ways. Before the throne there will be gathered together people speaking every imaginable language—Swahili, Hindi, English, German, Russian, and Slavic languages. Even languages that have long since died out will be heard once again before the throne of God, and all will be declaring together that Jesus Christ is Lord, to the glory of God the Father.

. . . BECAUSE THEY WILL NOT
BELIEVE UNLESS WE PREACH

Having pointed to the glorious comprehensiveness of God's plan of salvation, Paul then turns to the means by which God has determined to carry out the salvation of the world.

> For "everyone who calls on the name of the Lord will be saved." But how are they to call on him in whom they have not believed? And how are they to believe in him of whom they have never heard? And how are they to hear without someone preaching? And how are they to preach unless they are sent? As it is written, "How beautiful are the feet of those who preach the good news!"
>
> —ROMANS 10:13–15

Paul here lays out a logic of gospel proclamation, an unbreakable chain of cause and effect. If all who call upon the name of the Lord will be saved, then obviously they must believe in the one upon whom they are calling. But it is impossible that they should believe in someone of whom they have never heard, and they will not hear unless someone tells them—that is, unless someone *preaches* to them. This is how the church will fulfill the Great Commission and see the gathering of that great multitude before the throne. If we preach the gospel of Jesus, the world will hear it. And when they hear, some will believe in Him, call on His name, and be saved. Paul's great summary of this call to preach comes in verse 17: "So faith comes from hearing, and hearing through the word of Christ." Faith comes by hearing, and what they hear is the preaching of the Word.

It is important that we recognize that this is not just about words entering the ear. Jesus spoke about this in the parable of the sower and the soils in Matthew 13. There are people with perfectly good physical ears who nevertheless cannot truly hear the message of the gospel. On the other hand, there are those whose physical ears do not function at all who yet perceive and believe the gospel when it is communicated to them. So this is finally a matter of hearing with the heart. The point is not merely to hear the sounds of various words but to hear and receive the truth of the gospel.

THE PRIVILEGE OF THE PREACHER

What a high privilege it is to be a preacher of the gospel of Jesus Christ. Our Lord has given us the honor, the calling, the stewardship, and the commission of preaching a saving gospel to a world that is in desperate need of salvation—and all to the end that Jesus would be worshiped as Savior in every tongue, from every tribe and people and nation.

Looking at Paul's sense of urgency in the book of Romans, we are confronted with a direct challenge. Do we really believe that the world needs to hear the message of the gospel? Do we really believe that the gospel saves? Do we really believe that faith comes by hearing the Word of God? If so, then our minds should be filled with no more urgent desire than to preach. This is not an option for us or for the church. It is our commission.

CHAPTER 10

ON PREACHING TO DRY BONES

An Encouragement to Preachers

Since the Lord established His church, there have been preachers—lots of preachers. Through all its centuries of existence, the church has heard good preachers and it has endured bad preachers. It has gloried in faithful preachers and lamented faithless preachers. It has listened with rapt attention to masters of eloquence, and it has wondered at the loquacity of pulpit babblers. Humorists and bawlers, expositors and storytellers, thematic preachers, evangelistic preachers, literary preachers, sawdust preachers, postmodern preachers, seeker-seeking preachers, famous preachers, infamous preachers—the church has had them all.

All told, it must add up to millions and millions of hours of preaching—and listening. From the first century until now, the act of preaching represents a massive investment of human time, energy, and attention. And to what end? The millions of hours of preaching . . . so what? The typical preacher may sound like Martin Luther or

Charles Spurgeon on Sunday, but more often than not he feels like Solomon in Ecclesiastes on Monday morning: "Vanity! Vanity! All is vanity!"

The task of preaching often feels like a striving after the wind, and we often sympathize with the preacher in Ecclesiastes who laments, "What is crooked cannot be made straight, and what is lacking cannot be counted" (Ecclesiastes 1:15).

Furthermore, this work of preaching has a nasty way of getting one into trouble. It seems that the more faithful one is in preaching, the more trouble one encounters. You preach the Word, you speak the truth of the Scriptures, and the next thing you know, you are on the front page of the newspaper, or sitting in front of a group of agitated deacons or elders; even the youth group is up in arms about whatever you said.

Conflict and controversy are always hard, and it often seems that they are almost directly correlated with faithfulness in preaching. The harder you work at faithfully preaching the Word of God to your people, the greater the risk you endure.

If there is no controversy in your ministry, there is probably very little content to your preaching.

Preachers are sometimes even ejected and fired from their pulpits. That is simply one of the realities of the preaching ministry. Sometimes the preaching of the Word is met with antipathy and resistance—even by church members. Why? Because "the word of God is living and active, sharper than any two-edged sword, piercing to the division of soul and of spirit, of joints and of marrow, and discerning the thoughts and intentions of the heart" (Hebrews 4:12). This means that sometimes God uses the Word to rebuke and correct His people, and unavoidably it is the preacher who must speak that word and reap the response.

Indeed, I will go so far as to assert that if you are at peace with the world, you have abdicated your calling. You have become a court preacher to some earthly power, no matter how innocuous it might appear. To put it simply, you have been bought! If there is no controversy in your ministry, there is probably very little content to your preaching. The content of the Word of God is not only alive and active, but it is sharper than any two-edged sword, which means that it often does some surgery. By God's grace, the surgery leads to healing, but the cutting always comes first, and that leads to controversy.

PERSEVERING IN OUR PREACHING

Perhaps no one understood this better than the apostle Paul himself, who finally became a martyr for the sake of the gospel he preached. In giving his final instructions to Timothy, Paul spoke of being poured out as a libation, of being offered as an offering. The sufferings that Paul endured—beatings, stonings, shipwreck—all would be realized finally in martyrdom.

Thus Paul is emphatically aware of the dynamic of which we are speaking. As an apostle, he understands the very real experience of preaching. He understands the frustration, and he endures it. But even more, as we have already seen, he seems to revel in it, to celebrate it. Paul seems to understand that all the frustrations, conflict, controversy, and trouble of preaching are part of his calling and even part of the way God has determined that he will fulfill that calling. "Bring it on," Paul seems to say. "This is what I was made for. This is what I was called to do. This is what I am here for. Let's get at it!"

It cannot be a fierce determination alone, however, that strengthens us for the lifelong work of preaching. The stakes are much too high and the perils much too deadly for that. Instead, our perseverance in the task of preaching must be based on God's promise that He will, by His own power, make the preaching of His Word effective. It was through the prophet Isaiah that God said, "So shall my word be that goes out from my mouth; it shall not return to me empty, but it shall accomplish that which I purpose, and shall succeed in the thing for which I sent it" (Isaiah 55:11). And Paul confessed that though the gospel might be thought foolishness by those who do not believe, "it pleased God through the folly of what we preach to save those who believe" (1 Corinthians 1:21). We preach, not because we have come to the conclusion that preaching is the most rational or most effective means of reaching the lost, but because God has commanded it—and because He has promised to take that which the world would say is foolishness, and use it to save sinners.

A PARABLE FOR MODERN MINISTRY

God gave the prophet Ezekiel an incredible object lesson about this truth, which is recorded in Ezekiel 37. This is a text that has something particularly important to say to us about our calling to preach the gospel in this moment of history. Indeed, I believe this story of the dry bones presents us with a parable for ministry in our time.

> The hand of the Lord was upon me, and he brought me out in the Spirit of the Lord and set me down in the middle of the valley; it was full of bones. And he led me around among them, and behold, there were very many on the surface of the valley, and behold, they were very dry. And he said to me, "Son of man, can these bones live?" And I answered, "O Lord God, you know." Then he said to me, "Prophesy over these bones, and say to them, O dry bones, hear the word of the Lord. Thus says the Lord God to these bones: Behold, I will cause breath to enter you, and you shall live. And I will lay sinews upon you, and will cause flesh to come upon you, and cover you with skin, and put breath in you, and you shall live, and you shall know that I am the Lord."
>
> So I prophesied as I was commanded. And as I prophesied, there was a sound, and behold, a rattling, and the bones came together, bone to its bone. And I looked, and behold, there were sinews on them, and flesh had come upon them, and skin had covered them. But there was no breath in them. Then he said to me, "Prophesy to

the breath; prophesy, son of man, and say to the breath, Thus says the Lord God: Come from the four winds, O breath, and breathe on these slain, that they may live." So I prophesied as he commanded me, and the breath came into them, and they lived and stood on their feet, an exceedingly great army.

Then he said to me, "Son of man, these bones are the whole house of Israel. Behold, they say, 'Our bones are dried up, and our hope is lost; we are clean cut off.' Therefore prophesy, and say to them, Thus says the Lord God: Behold, I will open your graves and raise you from your graves, O my people. And I will bring you into the land of Israel. And you shall know that I am the Lord, when I open your graves, and raise you from your graves, O my people. And I will put my Spirit within you, and you shall live, and I will place you in your own land. Then you shall know that I am the Lord; I have spoken, and I will do it, declares the Lord."

—EZEKIEL 37:1–14

What an incredible text, and—if we are honest—what a bizarre story! The book of Ezekiel is filled with stories like these—stark imagery, stark language, unforgettable narrative—so much that Ezekiel himself has earned something of a reputation for strangeness. Daniel Block, in his two-volume commentary on Ezekiel, recounts how some scholars have tried to psychologize Ezekiel in order to figure out what kind of man sees visions like these and does the strange things that Ezekiel did. Block writes:

Not surprisingly, Ezekiel has been the subject of numerous psychoanalytical studies. While prophets were known often to act and speak erratically for rhetorical purposes, Ezekiel is in a class of his own. The concentration of so many bizarre features in one individual is without precedent: his muteness; lying bound and naked; digging holes in the walls of houses; emotional paralysis in the face of his wife's death; "spiritual" travels; images of strange creatures, of eyes, and of creeping things; hearing voices and the sounds of water; withdrawal symptoms; fascination with feces and blood; wild literary imagination; pornographic imagery; unreal if not surreal understanding of Israel's past; and the list goes on. It is no wonder that Karl Jaspers found in Ezekiel an unequalled case for psychological analysis. E.C. Broome concludes that Ezekiel was a true psychotic, capable of great religious insight but exhibiting a series of diagnostic characteristics: catatonia, narcissistic-masochistic conflict, schizophrenic withdrawal, delusions of grandeur and of persecution. In short, he suffered from a paranoid condition common in many great spiritual leaders.[1]

> We live in the middle of a valley of bones so dry and dead they do not even rattle.

Block goes on to point out that the psychoanalytic approach has largely been rejected, but there are still some who show a psychological fascination with Ezekiel. As Block notes, "D. J. Halperin attributes extraordinary features of Ezekiel's prophesy to an unconscious but overwhelming rage against females, who he perceives as cruel and powerful, seductive and treacherous, and a more deeply buried rage against male figures because of some abuse as a child."[2] All of that misses the point entirely. Here is how Block concludes:

One cannot deny the uniqueness of Ezekiel's style of ministry. But to attribute this uniqueness to a pathology arising from early abuse and an Oedipus complex misconstrues the profundity of his message and the sensitivity of his personality. His prophetic experiences, symbolic actions, and oracular pronouncements derive from encounters with God that have affected his entire being but were all directly related to his ministry. What other prophets spoke of, Ezekiel suffers. He is a man totally possessed by the Spirit of Yahweh, called, equipped, and gripped by the hand of God. Ezekiel is a *mopet*, "sign, portent" carrying in his body the oracles he proclaims and redefining the adage, "The medium is the message."[3]

That was Ezekiel—a pulpit committee's nightmare, but a prophet of God nonetheless. Ezekiel used unconventional methods in his ministry. He received unconventional visions, used unconventional language, and combined it all in an unconventional style. But then he was living in an unconventional age—and so are we.

If there is any one biblical image that comes most readily to my mind as a fitting description of our times, it is a valley of dry bones. This entire culture, left to us in the aftermath and debris of modernity, is a valley of dry bones. Intellectually, culturally, spiritually, and relationally, we live in the middle of a valley of bones so dry and dead they do not even rattle.

EZEKIEL'S VISION

In verses 1–2, the Lord calls to Ezekiel and takes him to a valley where He shows him a remarkable sight—a valley full of bones, described in verse 2 as being "very many" and "very dry." Before pressing ahead any further, we must be aware of the ancient Hebrew concern for the burial of the dead. The human body was to be respected, which meant that the remains of those deceased were treated very carefully. For such a massive number to die and for their bodies to lie exposed, their bones lying uncovered and desiccated on a valley floor, would have been the sign of utter destruction, utter death, utter hopelessness, degradation, and defeat.

No picture could more graphically communicate to Ezekiel's mind the idea of death, despair, and destruction than a valley full of dry bones. Not only so, but Ezekiel would also have been immediately reminded of the covenant curses in the Pentateuch. Much earlier Moses had warned the people:

> The Lord will cause you to be defeated before your enemies. You shall go out one way against them and flee seven ways before them. And you shall be a horror to all the kingdoms of the earth. And your dead body shall be food for all birds of the air and for the beasts of the earth, and there shall be no one to frighten them away.
> —DEUTERONOMY 28:25–26

Even as Moses was preparing the children of Israel to enter the Promised Land, he told them that if they would obey the Lord, they would be blessed; no army would be able to stand against them. But if they denied the Lord, disobeying Him and ignoring His statutes, then God's judgment would come upon them and they would be made a public reproach among the nations. They would be carried away in utter destruction, their army defeated and their carcasses given over to the birds of the air for food. Again, in Deuteronomy 28:36, Moses said to the Israelites: "The Lord will bring you and your king whom you set over you to a nation that neither you nor your fathers have known. And there you shall serve other gods of wood and stone." And in verse 45: "All these curses shall come upon you and pursue you and overtake you till you are destroyed, because you did not obey the voice of the Lord your God, to keep his commandments and his statutes that he commanded you."

Now, as Ezekiel surveys the valley of dry bones, all this has come to pass. The Israelites have been carried away into exile in Babylon, and their king has been dethroned and placed in the service of the king of the Chaldeans.

This vision of the dry bones is no less arresting to us than it was to Ezekiel. We live, as he did, in an era of spiritual death. The rebellion of humanity against God has now progressed so far that most cannot even remember the God they chose to disregard and disobey. Among so many in this culture, the judgment of God is seen even in people's ignorance that they are ignorant. Our culture is surviving on the residue of a Christian worldview—a culture that now thinks of God as no more than a nice concept.

Even among our churches, there are many in whom the scent of death is present. Statistics indicate that between 70 and 80 percent of our churches have plateaued or are declining in attendance. Even worse, many churches are not only in decline but also in spiritual dissipation. Entire denominations are in confusion and compromise or even worse. Lacking spiritual energy, devoid of biblical knowledge and conviction, many of our churches wear the pallor of death. Spiritually, our culture has wasted away to nothing—nothing but a valley of dry, desiccated bones.

GOD'S QUESTION AND EZEKIEL'S ANSWER

Death is death . . . isn't it? Dry bones are dry bones. They have no life nor any potential for life. No one stumbles upon a valley of dry bones and sets up camp to see what is going to happen next. There is no next. Nothing is going to happen . . . or is it?

In Ezekiel 37:3, the Lord God presents Ezekiel with a question: "Son of man, can these bones live?"

Talk about a final exam! What does one do with a question like that? The Lord God had brought the prophet to this awful place, showed him this awful vision—the arid, dusty floor of a valley covered in bones so lifeless that even the buzzards no longer circle above them—and then asks him, incredibly, "Son of man, can these bones live?"

What would Ezekiel have thought in that moment? Almost certainly, he knew of the miracles performed by Elijah and Elisha, the way they had raised people from the dead. But those resurrections from the dead were of persons whose bodies were very much present—flesh was still on the bones, life had just passed, breath had just moments ago filled their lungs. This was altogether different. One could not even tell which bone had been connected to another, nor how many bodies these scattered bones represented. And Ezekiel is asked by God, "Can these bones live?"

How would he answer? With conjecture? Speculation? Guess?

Cowardice? Doubt? Sometimes our entire theology is put on the line by one question. Imagine Jesus turning to His disciples and asking, "But who do you say that I am?" For the disciples seated around Jesus, everything came down to the atomic compactness of that one question and Peter's answer: "You are the Christ, the Son of the living God" (Matthew 16:15–16). One question and one answer—right or wrong, death or life, hope or hopelessness. Peter and John, too, standing before the Sanhedrin, got it right: "Whether it is right in the sight of God to listen to you rather than to God, you must judge, for we cannot but speak of what we have seen and heard" (Acts 4:19–20). Martin Luther, at the Diet of Worms, got it right: "My conscience is captive to the Word of God."

> Ezekiel's answer represents utter trust, mixed with humility and wisdom . . . a paradigm for how we also must answer.

Ezekiel also got it right—just right. He knew Deuteronomy 32:39, where the Lord says, "See now that I, even I, am he, and there is no god beside me; I kill and I make alive; I wound and I heal; and there is none that can deliver out of my hand." And he answered the question in a way that showed his complete trust in the sovereignty and holiness of God. He put the question back into the hands of the One who gives life: "O Lord God, you know."

Ezekiel's answer represents utter trust, mixed with humility and wisdom. As such, it becomes a paradigm for how we also must answer. In this age of postmodern confusion, spiritual death, cultural dissipation, and churchly confusion, the question comes to us too. Can these bones live? This is not an academic question for us who would preach God's Word. If the bones cannot live, if God cannot breathe life into that which is dead, then our preaching is in vain. Yet week after week, as we step into the pulpit and preach the gospel, we say with Ezekiel in faith, "O Lord God, you know whether these bones can live."

EZEKIEL'S SERMON

What the Lord next demands of Ezekiel is nothing short of astonishing. "Preach to these bones," He demands. We mentioned earlier that Ezekiel would have been the nightmare of any pulpit committee. That may be so, but this congregation is the nightmare of any preacher! The Lord was calling Ezekiel to stand before this pile of dry bones and preach to them, a calling that most people would say is utterly irrational. Preach to dry bones? It's insane. After all, no one expects life to come out of death. Yet that is what the Lord demands: "Then he said to me, 'Prophesy over these bones, and say to them, O dry bones, hear the word of the Lord.'"

Dry bones? Hear? Do dry bones hear?

Yes, sometimes they do. Even in the face of such a seemingly irrational demand, Ezekiel preaches. His faith issues in obedience, and he preaches. "So I prophesied as I was commanded," Ezekiel says, "and as I prophesied, there was a sound, and behold, a rattling, and the bones came together, bone to its bone." Imagine the sound of that rattling—bone reattaching to bone. Something is happening, something unprecedented, something supernatural, something miraculous. Ezekiel goes on: "And I looked, and behold, there were sinews on them, and flesh had come upon them, and skin had covered them." What we see here is the reversal of the process of decomposition, the undoing of what had happened on the floor of this valley. Originally there was a body whose skin disappeared, and then the flesh was eaten away and the bones fell apart. But now, the bones reassemble, sinews grow back on them, and flesh reappears.

Even after all this, Ezekiel sees that everything is still not right. "But there was no breath in them," he says. There was a hint of life, but no life—a valley of human bodies, but no breath. "Then he said to me, 'Prophesy to the breath; prophesy, son of man, and say to the breath, Thus says the Lord God: Come from the four winds, O breath, and breathe on these slain, that they may live.' So I prophesied as he commanded me, and the breath came into them, and they lived and stood on their feet, an exceedingly great army" (verses 8–10). Thus we see the gift of life, given by God through the power of His Word.

We must be careful here to see what God was teaching His people through this prophecy. Verse 11 makes it plain: "These bones are the whole house of Israel," bones whose "hope is lost." God calls upon Ezekiel to restore hope:

> Prophesy, and say to them, Thus says the Lord God: Behold, I will open your graves and raise you from your graves, O my people. And I will bring you into the land of Israel. And you shall know that I am the Lord, when I open your graves, and raise you from your graves, O my people. And I will put my Spirit within you, and you shall live, and I will place you in your own land. Then you shall know that I am the Lord; I have spoken, and I will do it, declares the Lord.
> —EZEKIEL 37:12–14

This is about the future hope of the resurrection. It is about God's promise to His own people that He would give them new life. Of course, this prophecy took place in a specific moment in Israel's history, and it was first directed to that reality—a different time and context from our own. But like every text in the Old Testament, this prophecy is fulfilled in Christ. Ultimately, its great hope is not limited to national Israel. This is the hope of the church— restoration and resurrection through the preached gospel of Jesus Christ.

> Our calling [is] to preach the Word . . . even to dry bones. This story of the bones . . . reminds us that God glories in bringing life out of death.

As we too survey the valley of dry bones in which we live, the Lord God asks each of us the same question: Can these dead bones live? And we must give an answer. What do you do when you pastor a church that no longer even remembers what a church is? What happens when you arrive on a field of ministry, or plant a new church, and there seems to be no life? What do you do in a season of spiritual deadness, or in a place where the deadness of postmodern ambiguity has set in?

In our valley of dry bones, there are many churches that have forgotten their first love and that desperately need a fresh wind of revival and reformation. So many churches need a reaffirmation of the faith and a recapturing of the life of the gospel. That is our context today, and we have to believe that the Lord will once again, to His glory, bring life out of death.

What will it take for that to happen? It is not merely incidental that the Lord God brought life to the bones through preaching. "Prophesy!" He said to Ezekiel. "Preach!" That is our calling, to preach the Word in season and out of season, to preach even to dry bones. Above all, this story of the bones testifies to the power and the sovereignty of God. It reminds us that God glories in bringing life out of death. In fact, that is the very essence of the gospel we preach. It is the hope of our calling. So let this story invigorate you and excite you. Let it simultaneously humble you, re-center you, and make you more serious about this task of preaching. Let it fuel in you a desire to hear the rattling and to see bones come to life.

People often ask me, "Are you hopeful?" And the answer is yes, I am hopeful. I am not optimistic. Christians have no right to be optimistic, but at the same time we have no right *not* to be hopeful. Optimism is a belief that things are finally going to end up happy. Hope, on the other hand, means that we know the Lord God of all creation, who sits in the heavens and rules over all the peoples of the earth. We know His grace. We know His mercy. We know His holiness, His character, and His love. Above all, we know His Son, and thus we live in hope.

I believe this is a great time to be alive, and a great time to be a preacher of the gospel of Jesus Christ. In His sovereignty, God has put us in this place at this time. He has given us this valley, filled—yes—with dry bones, but filled also with incredible promise.

No doubt, the challenges are great, and the frustrations are sometimes even greater. But we do not preach because we thought it would be easy. We preach because our hearts are broken by the spiritual death and destruction all around us—and because we see the spark of hope in the question our sovereign, life-giving God put to Ezekiel and now puts to us: "Son of man, can these bones live?" So we answer as he did, with simple faith and deep trust:

"O Lord God, You know."

A PASSION FOR PREACHING

Charles Haddon Spurgeon

In the midst of the theologically discredited nineteenth century, There was a preacher who had at least six thousand people in his congregation every Sunday, whose sermons for many years were cabled to New York every Monday and reprinted in the leading newspapers of the country, and who occupied the same pulpit for almost forty years without any diminishment in the flowing abundance of his preaching and without ever repeating himself or preaching himself dry.

"The fire he thus kindled, and turned into a beacon that shone across the seas and down through generations, was no mere brush fire of sensationalism, but an inexhaustible blaze that glowed and burned on solid hearths and was fed by the wells of the eternal Word. Here was the miracle of a bush that burned with fire and yet was not consumed."[1]

Thus commented Helmut Thielicke on the greatest Victorian preacher and one of the greatest princes of the pulpit to serve the church in any age: Charles Haddon Spurgeon.

It's no exaggeration to say Spurgeon was a legend in his own day: His became a household name in London before the preacher reached the age of twenty. His popularity has continued into the twenty-first century, and his voluminous writings are still among the best-selling devotional and homiletical materials currently available. What can explain this phenomenon? The Victorian age was noted as an era of princely preachers, and London—with the British Empire then at its height—was the setting for many of the greatest pulpit ministries in the history of the church. Spurgeon, however, stands alone as the most widely appreciated and influential preacher of his century. It was his passion for preaching that marked this man for God's blessing as a preacher.

A SPIRITUAL URGENCY

The background of Spurgeon's life is unremarkable. Born June 19, 1834, at Kelvedon in Essex, Spurgeon was the son and grandson of Congregational ministers. Spurgeon's father, John Spurgeon, was what would now be known as a bi-vocational preacher, serving in a largely itinerant ministry. But Charles's grandfather, James Spurgeon, was a well-known Congregational minister. Charles spent most of his childhood in his grandfather's manse at Stambourne, where he was exposed to a warmhearted devotion and to his grandfather's extensive library of Puritan theology.

The Spurgeon family noticed early a particular sense of spiritual urgency in young Charles, and the parish manse was a healthy place for Spurgeon to indulge in rather precocious theological investigations. The catalyst for his theological development was his grandfather's library of Puritan classics. In an attic loft, Spurgeon spent many boyhood days in the company of Richard Sibbes, John Owen, Richard Baxter, and John Bunyan—especially Bunyan.

Spurgeon's disquietude was not eased until January 6, 1850, when he was converted during a meeting at the Primitive Methodist chapel at Colchester. His testimony of that day was of a burden released. As he would write in his autobiography: "The frown of God no longer resteth upon me; but my Father smiles, I can see His eyes—they are glancing love; I hear His voice—it is full of sweetness. I am forgiven, I am forgiven, I am forgiven!"[2] Spurgeon was soon to join a Baptist church, driven to the conviction of believer's baptism by his own study of the Bible.

Within a matter of months, Spurgeon would preach his first sermon, tricked into doing so by an older friend who asked him to go to a Teversham cottage the next Sunday evening, for a young man was to preach there for the first time and would be glad to have the company. "That was a cunningly devised sentence," Spurgeon later wrote, for "a request to go and preach would have met with a decided negative, but merely to act as company to a good brother who did not like to be lonely, and perhaps might ask us to give out a hymn or to pray, was not at all a difficult matter, and the request, understood in that fashion, was cheerfully complied with." Spurgeon relates the story:

Our Sunday-school work was over, and tea had been taken, and we set off through Barnwell, and away along the Newmarket-road, with a gentleman some few years our senior. We talked of good things, and at last we expressed our hope that he would feel the presence of God while preaching. He seemed to start, and assured us that he had never preached in his life, and could not attempt such a thing: he was looking to his young friend, Mr. Spurgeon, for that. This was a new view of the situation, and I could only reply that I was no minister, and that even if I had been I was quite unprepared. My companion only repeated that *he*, even in a more emphatic sense, was not a preacher, that he would help *me* in any other part of the service, but that there would be no sermon unless I gave them one.

Praying to God as he walked along the road, Spurgeon resolved to make an attempt. "It seemed a great risk and a serious trial; but depending upon the power of the Holy Ghost, I would at least tell out the story of the cross, and not allow the people to go home without a word."[3]

That would be Spurgeon's practice and pledge for the remainder of his remarkable ministry. By the next year, Spurgeon had been called as pastor of a small chapel at Waterbeach, where his reputation soon expanded throughout the Cambridgeshire area. In 1853, his reputation took him to the pulpit of the famed New Park Street Baptist Church in London.

The New Park Street Baptist Church had once been numbered among London's most famous and well-attended churches. Previous pastors had included Benjamin Keach, John Gill, and John Rippon. But the twelve-hundred-seat sanctuary held only about one hundred when Spurgeon arrived to preach a guest sermon. Within eighteen months of Spurgeon's arrival, however, the congregation would be forced into the cavernous Exeter Hall in order to accommodate the thousands who came to hear their preacher. The scene would shift in 1861 to the newly constructed Metropolitan Tabernacle in south London, where Spurgeon would draw a congregation of no less than six thousand persons for thirty years.

Charles Spurgeon's unprecedented ministry defies summarization, but one homiletical resource states it in stark terms: "Before he was twenty a significant church in London called him as pastor. Within two years he was preaching to audiences of 10,000 people; at twenty-two he was the most popular preacher of his day. By the time he was twenty-seven, a church seating 6,000 people had been built to accommodate the crowds which flocked to hear him preach. For over thirty years he pastored the same church without decrease in power or appeal."[4]

Indeed, Spurgeon dominated the pulpit of his age like a Colossus, with his services drawing thousands and his printed sermons hitting the streets within hours of their pulpit delivery. Even today, Charles Haddon Spurgeon tops virtually every list of the most famous and influential preachers of the English-speaking world. And more than a century after his death, thousands of his sermons remain in print and in demand. What can explain the power and substance of this ministry?

A PASSION FOR EXPOSITION
AND PROCLAMATION

The defining characteristic of Spurgeon's ministry is precisely what is missing from so many pulpits today—an undiluted passion for the exposition and proclamation of God's Word. The question is, *Can that passion be recovered?*

Spurgeon was, it must be granted, a particularly effective preacher. His voice was often described as "silvery" in its effect and intonation. Indeed his voice was powerful enough to be heard clearly by as many as twenty thousand persons without amplification. Spurgeon preached to an estimated ten million persons during his ministry—all before the invention of radio and television. Once, when testing the acoustics of London's spacious Agricultural Hall, Spurgeon shouted, "Behold the Lamb of God which taketh away the sins of the world." A workman would later tell Spurgeon that he had heard the words while working in the rafters, and had been led to faith in Christ. As described by Harwood Pattison, "His voice was a powerful organ. Its first note, while it filled with ease the largest room, was so personal that each one of his hearers seemed to be especially addressed. . . . It was clarion in its powers to arouse, and lacked only a pathetic note to make it perfect."[5] But Spurgeon's voice, though unique, was not the secret of his pulpit power. A great many other Victorian divines were blessed with powerful voice boxes and gifts of inflection.

The popular appeal of Spurgeon's preaching could be traced, in part, to his unique method of crafting messages that were at once both rich in substance and clear in presentation. Spurgeon rejected the highbrow elegance of the aristocratic Victorians and preached using popular language and directness. He used illustrations from everyday life and current events, rather than the literary allusions common in Victorian sermons. This approach had an immediate impact in London, starved for relevant preaching. "Not for a long time," one observer noted, "had a prominent preacher condescended to preach the simple gospel in plain English, free from classical quotations and over-burdened rhetoric."[6] Spurgeon instructed his student preachers to read the Bible and the newspaper side by side, and he was a keen observer of his culture. Current events, he urged, illustrated timeless truths.

Spurgeon's popular style won him both friends and enemies. Much of the response fell along class lines. Spurgeon came to prominence in London as the Industrial Revolution was in full sway. A new middle class of entrepreneurs, shopkeepers, and managers was emerging, and those persons found Spurgeon's preaching compelling and understandable. They flocked to his services, joined by representatives of both the poor and the aristocratic. After observing the young Spurgeon, James Grant wrote in the *Morning Advertiser* that he "has evidently made George Whitefield his model, and, like that unparalleled preacher, that prince of pulpit orators, is very fond of striking apostrophes." Others were less taken with Spurgeon's approach. Older, more established ministers found the young upstart uncultured, at least in terms of current literature and classical references. Cartoons in the popular press portrayed Spurgeon as a young dynamo upsetting the comfort of the ensconced pulpit orators. Spurgeon was, in fact, accused of theatrical tactics and manipulation. However, no less than Helmut Thielicke, who observed Nazi propaganda and manipulation firsthand, absolved Spurgeon of such methods: "Charles Haddon Spurgeon . . . was still unaware of the wiles of propaganda . . . He worked only through the power of the Word which created its own hearers and changed souls."[7]

Spurgeon spoke with unusual directness and used references to everyday life. The *Ipswich Express* described Spurgeon's preaching as "redolent of bad taste, vulgar, and theatrical." But his style was vulgar only by the standards of Victorian aristocrats. For most Londoners, what the aristocracy described as "vulgar" was the stuff of everyday life. For his part, Spurgeon was undeterred: "I am perhaps vulgar, and so on, but it is not intentional, save that I must and will make the people listen. My firm conviction is that we have had quite enough polite preachers, and that 'the many' require a change. God has owned me among the most degraded and offcast. Let others serve their class; these are mine, and to them I must keep."[8]

Thielicke noted the "worldliness" of Spurgeon's sermons, even as he acknowledged the "homiletical risks" Spurgeon chose to take. "The dogmatician, the exegete, and also professor of practical theology may often be impelled to wield their blue pencils; the aesthete may often see red and the liturgiologists turn purple when they read his sermons and hear what he did. For the priests and the Levites always have the hardest time listening with simplicity and without bias." To Thielicke, this worldliness was the glory, not the scandal, of Spurgeon's preaching. "Such critics ought to see this man Spurgeon the shepherd who was willing to allow his robe—including his clerical robe—to be torn to tatters by thorns and sharp stones as he clambered after the lost sheep . . . Worldly preaching is impossible without having the earth leave its traces on a man's wardrobe. Here there are no robes that look as if they had just come out of a sandbox." Furthermore, Spurgeon's humor, said Thielicke, is "Easter laughter," the laughter that comes as a "mode of redemption because it is sanctified—because it grows out of an overcoming of the world. . . ."[9]

PREACHING POWER FOUNDED ON CONVICTION

But Spurgeon's homiletical method, revolutionary and effective though it was, was neither the foundation of his ministry nor the source of his power, any more than was the sound of his voice. The real foundation of his power was Christian conviction. Long before Charles Spurgeon was a great preacher, he was a great believer—a man possessed by deep passion for the Word of God and the gospel of Jesus Christ. Preaching was for him, therefore, first and foremost a matter of conviction, even before it blossomed into communication. While the Victorians often minimalized doctrine and the Tractarians taught their theory of doctrinal "reserve," Spurgeon preached a full-bodied gospel with substantive content and unashamed conviction. In this he was regarded as something of an exception, but he held fast to his biblical faith, Calvinist convictions, and evangelistic appeal.

"I take my text and make a bee-line to the cross," explained Spurgeon, and that brief statement is his preaching method in sum. He would often preach as many as five to seven sermons a week, but Sunday sermons at the Metropolitan Tabernacle consumed most of his energies in preparation. Spurgeon would seek texts for his Sunday sermons throughout the week, searching through prayer, Bible reading, and conversation with friends (especially his devoted wife, Susannah) to find the most appropriate text for Sunday's sermons. Then on Saturday night, he would sequester himself away from family and friends by six o'clock and remain in his study until the morning message was in outline form. From that outline, Spurgeon would preach an extemporaneous message lasting forty-five minutes to an hour, on average.

Spurgeon found the identification of the text his most vexing challenge, and it consumed much of his energies during the week. "A man who goes up and down from Monday morning until Saturday night, and indolently dreams that he is to have his text sent down by an angelic messenger in that last hour or two of the week, tempts God, and deserves to stand speechless on the Sabbath,"[10] he charged. His struggle is made clear in this reflective passage:

> I have often said that my greatest difficulty is to fix my mind upon the particular texts which are to be the subjects of discourse on the following day. . . . As soon as any passage of Scripture really grips my heart and soul I concentrate my whole attention upon it, look at the precise meaning of the original, closely examine the context so as to see the special aspect of the text in its surroundings, and roughly jot down all the thoughts that occur to me concerning the

subject, leaving to a later period the orderly marshalling of them for presentation to my hearers.[11]

But whatever the text—Old Testament or New Testament—Spurgeon would find his way to the gospel of the Savior on the cross. That gospel was put forth with the full force of substitutionary atonement and with warnings of eternal punishment but for the grace of God in Jesus Christ.

Spurgeon's uncompromising message was offensive to some even in Victorian England. Some even chose to admire Spurgeon's preaching ministry while ignoring or minimizing his theology. This Spurgeon would not allow. As Iain Murray states: "The only way to deal with Spurgeon's theology is to accept it or forget it: the latter is what I believe has largely happened in the twentieth century. And Spurgeon without his theology is about as distorted as the cheap china figures of Spurgeon which were offered for sale by charlatans more than a century ago."[12]

The famous preacher found himself engaged in several heated theological disputes, ranging from debates over baptismal regeneration to the infamous "Downgrade Controversy" of his final years. In each of these, he attempted to maintain clear evangelical conviction, while keeping the focus on the gospel. He resisted any compromise on substitutionary atonement, the authority and inspiration of Scripture, eternal punishment for unbelievers, original sin, and the absoluteness of Christianity.

The lack of emphasis on substitutionary atonement that marked many of his contemporaries troubled Spurgeon, for he saw no genuine gospel in any preaching that was embarrassed by the scriptural witness to what God in Christ did on behalf of the redeemed. As he stated: "I have always considered, with Luther and Calvin, that the sum and substance of the gospel lies in that word Substitution—Christ standing in the stead of man. If I understand the gospel, it is this: I deserve to be lost forever; the only reason why I should not be damned is this, that Christ was punished in my stead, and there is no need to execute a sentence twice for sin."[13]

To be sure, Spurgeon was concerned with the function and effectiveness of the sermon. A student at his famous pastor's college once asked how he could focus more clearly on bringing believers into the faith. "Do you expect converts every time you preach?" Spurgeon asked. The student quickly retorted, "Of course not." And the reply came back: "That is why you have none."[14] But Spurgeon made content his primary concern, trusting that God would use the substance of his message to penetrate the hearts of his hearers. "Sermons should have real teaching in them, and their doctrine should be solid, substantial, and abundant. We do not enter the pulpit to talk for talk's sake; we have instructions to convey, important to the last degree, and we cannot afford to utter pretty nothings."[15]

He warned his students to evaluate their sermons by content, not by structure or design. "To divide a sermon well may be a very useful art, but how if there is nothing to divide? . . . The grandest discourse ever delivered is an ostentatious failure if the doctrine of the grace of God be absent from it; it sweeps over men's heads like a cloud, but it distributes no rain upon the thirsty earth; and therefore the remembrance of it to souls taught wisdom by an experience of pressing need is one of disappointment, or worse."

"Brethren," he pleaded, "weigh your sermons. Do not retail them by the yard, but deal them out by the pound. Set no store by the quantity of words which you utter, but try to be esteemed for the quality of your matter."[16]

Spurgeon held fast to Calvinist theology, even as he extended a universal appeal to sinners, calling them to repent and believe the gospel. When asked how he could reconcile his understanding of election and his evangelistic appeal, he retorted quickly: "I do not try to reconcile friends."

That quality of vigor and vitality produced one of the most remarkable ministries of the church in the modern age—or any age for that matter. Upon Spurgeon's death, Texan B. H. Carroll was moved to deliver an address celebrating his British colleague's life and ministry: "With whom among men can you compare him? He combined the preaching power of Jonathan Edwards and Whitefield with the organizing power of Wesley, and the energy, fire, and courage of Luther. In many respects he was most like Luther. In many, most like Paul."[17] Despite the acclaim he received, Spurgeon never intended to be the center of attention, in life or in death. He would point to the cross. As Thielicke stated plainly, "His message never ran dry because he was never anything but a recipient."[18] Spurgeon would be quick to affirm Thielicke's point. He preached the grace of God with such power because he had experienced the grace of God.

In our era, distanced by more than a century from Charles Spurgeon, we would do well to remember this great man and the impact of his ministry. Beyond this, we should be reminded of the centrality of biblical confidence and theological conviction to the preaching task. Where are the Spurgeons of this generation?

NOTES

Preface: The State of Preaching Today

1. John A. Broadus, *On the Preparation and Delivery of Sermons,* 4th Ed. Revised by Vernon L. Stanfield (San Francisco: Harper Collins, 1979), 3.

Chapter 1: Preaching as Worship

1. A. W. Tozer, *Tozer on Worship and Entertainment: Selected Excerpts* (Camp Hill, PA: Christian Publications, 1997), 104-105.

2. A. W. Tozer, *Man: The Dwelling Place of God* (Harrisburg, PA: Christian Publications, 1966), 136.

3. Kent Hughes, *Disciplines of a Godly Man* (Wheaton, IL: Crossway, 2001), 110.

4. Elmer Towns, *Putting an End to Worship Wars* (Nashville: Broadman & Holman, 1996), 5.

5. Roger Scruton, *The Aesthetics of Music* (Oxford, UK: Oxford Univ. Press, 1999), 460.

6. George Hunter III, *Church for the Unchurched* (Nashville: Abingdon Press, 1996), 59.

7. A. W. Tozer, *Rut, Rot . . . Revival* (Camp Hill, PA: Christian Publications, 1992), 172–73.

8. Marin Luther, *Works,* vol. 16 "Lectures on Isaiah 1–39," Trans. Herman J. A. Bouman (St. Louis: Concordia, 1969), 73.

9. From the editor's preface to John R. W. Stott, *Between Two Worlds* (Eerdmans, 1982), 7.

Chapter 2: The Ground of Preaching

1. Carl F. H. Henry, *God, Revelation, and Authority*, vol. 2 (Crossway, 1999), 8.
2. John Calvin, *Commentary on the Book of Isaiah*, vol. 4, trans. William Pringle (Eerdmans, 1948), 172. From Calvin's commentary on Isaiah 55:11
3. John Calvin, *Institutes*, V.1.5, ed. John T. McNeill, trans. Ford Lewis Battles, (Louisville: Westminster John Knox, 2006), 1018.
4. James Denny, *Studies in Theology* (London: Hodder and Stoughton, 1895), 161.
5. Charles H. Spurgeon, "The Necessity of the Spirit's Work," *The New Park Street Pulpit, 1859–1860* (Pasadena, TX: Pilgrim Publications, 1975), 211.
6. Calvin, *Institutes*, V.II.ii.21, ed. McNeill.
7. Ibid., V.I.vii.4.
8. Martin Luther, *Werke*, vol. 52 (Weimar, 1915), 308–9 or in English, Ewald Martin Plass, ed., *What Luther Says: An Anthology* (St. Louis: Concordia, 1959), II:664.
9. Martyn Lloyd-Jones, *Preaching & Preachers* (Grand Rapids, MI: Zondervan, 1971), 325.
10. J. I Packer, "Authority in Preaching," in *The Gospel in the Modern World*, ed. Martyn Eden and David F. Wells (London: InterVarsity, 1991), 199.

Chapter 3: Preaching Is Expository

1. David F. Wells, *No place for Truth, or Whatever Happened to Evangelical Theology?* (Grand Rapids, MI: Eerdmans, 1993), 173.

Chapter 4: Expository Preaching

1. T. H. L. Parker, *Calvin's Preaching* (Edinburgh: T & T Clark, 1992), 79
2. Found at www.biblebb.com/files/macqa/IA-sermonapp.htm.
3. Richard Sennett, *Authority* (New York: Alfred A. Knopf, 1980), 15.
4. Willard Gaylin & Bruce Jennings, *The Perversion of Autonomy: Coercion & Constraints in a Liberal Society* (Washington, DC: Georgetown Univ. Press, 2003), 11.
5. Fred Craddock, *As One Without Authority* (Nashville: Abingdon Press, 1979), 13.
6. Ibid., 14–15.
7. Martyn Lloyd-Jones, *Authority* (Downers Grove, IL: InterVarsity, 1958), 10.
8. Charles Spurgeon, "The Call to the Ministry," in *Lectures to My Students* (Grand Rapids, MI: Zondervan, 1979), 27.

9. John Calvin, "Sermon on 2 Timothy 2:16–18," in R. Bentley, ed., *A Selection of the Most Celebrated Sermons of M. Luther and J. Calvin, Eminent Ministers of the Gospel, Etc.* (New York: Ludwig & Tolefree, 1829), 61.

10. Martin Luther, *Luther's Works*, ed. Jaroslav Pelikan, vol. 22 (St. Louis: Concordia, 1955), 528.

11. Hughes Oliphant Old, *The Reading and Preaching of the Scriptures in the Worship of the Christian Church* (Grand Rapids, MI: Eerdmans, 2007), 189.

Chapter 6: "Did Not Our Hearts Burn Within Us?"

1. Jean-Francois Lyotard, *The Postmodern Condition* (Minneapolis: Univ. of Minn. Press, 1984), xxiv.

Chapter 8: Stranger Than It Used to Be

1. Jean-Francois Lyotard, *The Postmodern Condition: A Report on Knowledge* (Minneapolis: Univ. of Minn. Press, 1984), xxiv.

2. See, for example, Jacques Derrida, *Of Grammatology*, trans. Gayatri Chakravorty Spivak (Baltimore: Johns Hopkins Univ. Press, 1997).

3. E. Michael Jones, *Degenerate Moderns: Modernity as Rationalized Sexual Misbehavior* (San Francisco: Ignatius Press, 1993).

4. Walter Truett Anderson, *Reality Isn't What It Used to Be* (San Francisco: Harper and Row, 1990), 188.

5. Robert Wuthnow, *After Heaven: Spirituality in America Since the 1950s* (Princeton, NJ: Princeton Univ. Press, 2005), 139.

6. John Calvin, *Institutes*, McNeill & Battles, vol. 1, 40.

Chapter 9: The Urgency of Preaching:

1. Richard Baxter, *Poetical Fragments,* "Love Breathing Thanks & Praise" (New York: Gregg Division of McGraw-Hill, 1971), 30.

Chapter 10: On Preaching to Dry Bones

1. Daniel I. Block, *The Book of Ezekiel* (Grand Rapids, MI: Eerdmans, 1998), 10.

2. Ibid.

3. Block, 11.

Epilogue: A Passion for Preaching

1. Helmut Thielicke, *Encounter with Spurgeon*, trans. John W. Doberstein (Cambridge, MA: James Clarke & Co., 1964), 1.

2. Charles Haddon Spurgeon, *Autobiography*, vol. 1 (Chicago: Fleming H. Revell Company, 1898), 110.

3. "Our First Sermon," *Sword and Trowel,* January 1880.

4. Clyde E. Fant Jr. and William M. Pinson, Jr., *20 Centuries of Great Preaching: An Encyclopedia of Preaching, vol. 6, Spurgeon to Meyer, 1834–1929* (Waco, TX: Word Books, 1971), 3.

5. T. Harwood Pattison, *The History of Christian Preaching* (Philadelphia: Baptist Publication Society, 1903), 335.

6. Charles Ray, *A Marvelous Ministry: The Story of C. H. Spurgeon's Sermons* (London: Passmore & Alabaster, 1905; reprinted Pasadena, TX: Pilgrim, 1985), 17.

7. Thielicke, 1.

8. Charles Haddon Spurgeon, "Letter," April 24, 1855. Available at www.home-church.com/spirituality/spurgeon–letters.html.

9. Thielicke, 40–41.

10. Charles Haddon Spurgeon, *Lectures to My Students* (Grand Rapids, MI: Zonder-van, 1979), 93.

11. Charles Haddon Spurgeon, *Autobiography*, vol IV, 66.

12. Iain Murray, *The Forgotten Spurgeon* (Carlisle, PA: Banner of Truth Trust, 1966), 5.

13. Charles Haddon Spurgeon, *Autobiography*, 113.

14. G. H. Pike, ed., *Speeches by C. H. Spurgeon, at Home and Abroad* (London: Pass-more & Alabaster, 1878), 85.

15. Charles Haddon Spurgeon, *Lectures to My Students* (Grand Rapids, MI: Zonder-van, 1979), 70.

16. Ibid., 70–71.

17. B. H. Carroll, "Memorial Address for C. H. Spurgeon," Minister's Institute, Nash-ville, TN, February 1892. Available at members.aol.com/pilgrimpub/deathchs.htm.

17. Thielicke, 1.

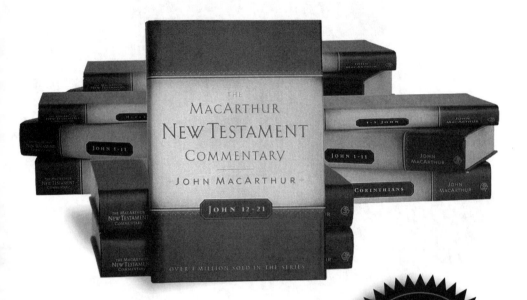

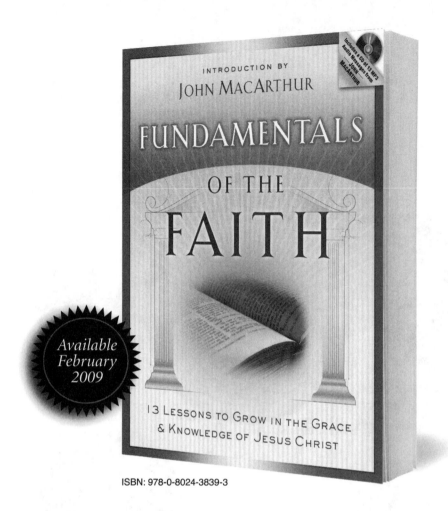

INTRODUCTION BY

JOHN MACARTHUR

FUNDAMENTALS

OF THE

FAITH

13 LESSONS TO GROW IN THE GRACE
& KNOWLEDGE OF JESUS CHRIST

Available February 2009

Includes a CD of 13 mp3 audio messages from JOHN MACARTHUR

ISBN: 978-0-8024-3839-3

"On Sunday mornings at Grace Community church, small groups of people gather together in 'Fundamentals of the Faith' classes to use this manual of thirteen lessons, which blend basic biblical truths with personal obedience and service." With topics ranging from "God: His Character and Attributes" to "The Church: Fellowship and Worship," *Fundamentals of the Faith* is an ideal study to disciple new believers or realize afresh what it means to believe in Jesus.

Fundamentals of the Faith contains a CD with 13 audio messages from John MacArthur to accompany each lesson.

Introduction by John MacArthur

Preorder your copy now at your favorite local or online bookstore.

www.MoodyPublishers.com
Sign up for Moody Publishers Book Club on our website.